$10

10509

Mon/85

THE THEATRE
OF
EMBARRASSMENT

THE THEATRE
OF
EMBARRASSMENT

Francis Wyndham

Chatto & Windus
LONDON

Published in 1991 by
Chatto & Windus Ltd
20 Vauxhall Bridge Road
London SW1V 2SA

A CIP catalogue record for this book is available from the
British Library

ISBN 0 7011 3726 6

Photoset in Linotron Palatino by
Rowland Phototypesetting Ltd
Bury St Edmunds, Suffolk
Printed in Great Britain by
Mackays of Chatham plc, Chatham, Kent

CONTENTS

INTRODUCTION

PEOPLE OFTEN FIND THEMSELVES, AS THEY GROW OLDER, DOING the very things that they had always insisted they would never do. In the past, when it was sometimes suggested that I might one day publish a selection of my journalistic pieces, I would grandly deride the idea. If such work was any good at all, I maintained, it was because it was right only for its moment; similar collections by other writers had often struck me as ill-judged. But I changed my mind when Carmen Callil happened to ask me if I would consider compiling a commonplace book for Chatto & Windus. She meant, of course, an anthology of my favourite passages from world literature – but I conceived the egotistic notion that the attractive exercise of personal choice could after all be restricted to items written entirely by myself. So that is what this book is: some articles, book reviews and interviews which I enjoyed rereading and which also seem to me now to have certain qualities in common beyond the mere fact of my authorship.

The earliest piece, on Alice Faye, was written in 1955 and delivered as a lecture at the avant-garde Institute of Contemporary Arts, then run by Lawrence Alloway, whose original and influential approach to aesthetics anticipated the whole Pop Art movement. The occasion (a memorable evening) was billed as a Symposium of Heroines. I was in good company. The eminent art critic, David Sylvester, spoke about Marilyn Monroe; the distinguished typographer, Toni del Renzio, discussed Audrey Hepburn; and the President of the Piper Laurie Fan Club gave the definitive talk on Piper Laurie. (This last contribution was unanimously judged to be the best.) Alloway himself was in the chair, so it was a crowded platform – in fact, the speakers almost outnumbered the audience, which was sparse. It was the first (and remains the last) time that I spoke in public and I was very nervous. Lucian Freud had tried to reassure me:'They'll all be cranks there anyhow, so it doesn't matter what you say, they're bound to think it wonderful.' I got through it somehow, with only one minor mishap when it was over. Instead of illustrating my lecture on Alice Faye with lantern slides, I had decided to play one of her records as a climax – but the machine was adjusted to the wrong speed and the opening notes of 'I've Got My Love to Keep Me Warm' emerged as the deepest bass, ludicrously exaggerating my claim that 'her voice was unusually low'.

At this time, I still thought of myself as an exclusively literary journalist (I had been reviewing books regularly since 1946) and would have been alarmed by an assignment involving on-the-spot reportage. What I really wanted to write was fiction. But throughout the 1960s and 1970s I did a number of interviews (mostly for the *The Sunday Times Magazine*) and this experience altered my perception of the relationship between journalism and 'creative writing'. When, in the 1980s, I did go back to writing fiction, I found that it had taught me some valuable lessons.

The main lesson was negative – what not to do. On most of these interviews I was accompanied by a photographer whose pictures would be at least as important an element of the published feature as my text – often, *more* important, for I was lucky enough to work with the best: Snowdon, Bailey, McCullin, Montgomery, Duffy, Donovan . . . So I understood that I was relieved of the laborious necessity of trying to describe what the subject, and his or her surroundings, *looked* like – that was the photographer's job. Mine was to do what he couldn't – to convey what the person *was* like. The simplest way of doing this was to get across as exactly as possible what the subject *sounded* like, and I believe one's first task as an interviewer should be to pay as close attention to individual habits of speech as to the meaning of what is said. (Inexplicably, I found that the use of a tape recorder, which might be expected to facilitate the working of this trick, actually inhibits it in practice.) Now, when reading a novel or story, I sometimes think that it might have benefited if the author had imagined a collaboration with some ghostly illustrator and could therefore refrain from attempting those purely physical descriptions which (except in rare moments of inspiration) are beyond the scope of words.

The photographer's presence at the interview helped in other ways. However experienced, he would usually be nervous: his success depended on capturing a definitive image within a comparatively short period of time, whereas I might have weeks in which to compose my article. The subject would usually be nervous, too – more of being photographed than of being questioned by me. Thus the photographic session created an atmosphere of dramatic tension to be succeeded by a feeling of relief during the interview itself – the whole process suggesting an audition for, and a rehearsal of, some scene in the theatre of embarrassment. This general sense of heightened self-consciousness aided me in my secret aim, which was to invest my account of the event (while inventing nothing and scrupulously sticking to objective fact) with the intensity and clear-cut shape of a good short story. Of course, this aim was never achieved – though I think I came close to it twice, in 'P. J. Proby' and in 'Mother and Son'.

These two pieces may need a note of explanation: Proby was a pop singer briefly notorious because his trousers had a habit of splitting on stage, and Vivienne (the subject of 'Mother and Son') was a highly successful 'society' photographer. I must confess to having chosen, for republication in this collection, those interviews which I hope reflect credit on my skill rather than those with easier, more famous subjects in whom interest would be automatic. I very seldom interviewed intellectuals, preferring the artless revelations of figures in the worlds of show business and fashion, but I did write profiles of several celebrities which are not included here, while some of the people featured in this book may now be forgotten and a few were always obscure.

At the height of Swinging London, in the days when Merlin could be sighted coming out of Waitrose in the King's Road, there was said to be a Martian working at Sanderson's wallpaper shop. Terence Stamp had spoken to him. David Bailey wanted to take this Martian's photograph and asked me to come along too and do the interview. For obvious reasons, this project never got off the ground, but I recall it as symptomatic of my approach to interviewing at that time. Each assignment seemed an amusing adventure on which one set out with little idea of what one would find but with an expectation of endless possibilities. Then, around 1980, I suddenly went off the whole thing and now the thought of having to conduct an interview (I do sometimes have nightmares in which I find myself back in that situation) fills me with dread.

Francis Wyndham, 1990

PART ONE
PERFORMANCE

THE THEATRE OF
EMBARRASSMENT

SUPPORTERS OF THE THEATRE OFTEN POINT OUT THAT, AS A medium, it has one great advantage over its rivals, the cinema screen and the printed page: it is 'live'. This means that at every performance there is a chance that something will go wrong. And that is just what the people in the audience half-consciously expect – as an exciting reward for all the irritating discomforts of theatregoing: the booking ahead, the disturbance of dinner, the awkward intervals and crowded bars, the general sense of *déplacement* when they could be at home reading, or watching a safely taped programme on television.

They get their reward. I have never been to the theatre without *some* mishap taking place: a bit of the scenery falls down, an actor forgets his lines and remains deaf to the all-too-audible prompter, a gunshot is heard either before or after a trigger is seen to be pressed. There is a whole *genre* of theatrical stories hinging on such disasters (John Barrymore's drunkenness, Mrs Patrick Campbell's practical jokes), and the true pro is judged as much by his or her *sang-froid* in the face of them as by any other proof of histrionic talent. While the spectators imagine that they are hoping to witness some actor give the greatest performance of his life, never to be repeated in exactly the same way, they are also wondering if he may not give the *worst*, or even refuse to give one at all. Hence all the subsidiary drama – more potent than any on stage – of last-minute broken legs and ill-rehearsed understudies; hence the magic incantation 'the show must go on' (which really means that perhaps it won't). When Judy Garland turned up late for a concert in Australia, refused to sing, lost contact with the orchestra and insulted the audience which then booed her, she was in a sense giving the performance of her career and her audience was privileged to be present at a great moment in theatrical history: that dreaded, longed-for moment when the show just jolly well *doesn't* go on. Embarrassment could go no further; and, as with any emotion carried beyond its limit, brings with it a sense of release.

The theatre of embarrassment does not only consist of failure, although this may be its more obvious aspect. I believe that the most successful theatrical experiences are also rooted in this emotion. What happens in a theatre? A group of people, strangers to one another, congregate at a given time within a large room. There – fidgeting, coughing, sneezing, sweating – they watch a (generally) smaller group of people walking about in a small space, narrowly avoiding collision with each other, speaking in unnaturally loud voices, visibly spitting, sometimes taking off their clothes, pretending to make love, to fight, to die. The people in the audience have paid money in the hope that they will be made to feel some emotion – pity, terror, mirth, lust, interest, sympathy, outrage. In circumstances as conducive as these to intense embarrassment, they very naturally feel embarrassed; relieved at feeling *something*, and therefore getting their money's worth, they mistake the shock of embarrassment for whatever emotion the play is intended to inspire. That physical feeling of interior shrinking described as 'curling up inside' becomes 'shivers down the spine'; 'I didn't know where to look' is translated into a pricking of the eyes or finds relief in nervous laughter; in fact, the spectator who believes himself uplifted by displays of theatrical virtuosity is really going through the floor.

The middlebrow theatre (and the theatre is essentially a middlebrow phenomenon) has grasped this elementary confusion, and consists entirely of plays designed as straightforward vehicles of embarrassment. The best English actresses have always shone in these. Peggy Ashcroft in *The Deep Blue Sea*, as a cultured lady physically attracted to a common young man; Flora Robson stealing a nightdress in *Black Chiffon*, and then being told that she is subconsciously jealous of her son's marriage; Wendy Hiller getting drunk in *Waters of the Moon*, and blurting out her loneliness; Celia Johnson's tremulous breakdown in *Flowering Cherry*: all were master performances in the tricky art of inducing enjoyable embarrassment. These excellent actresses have also appeared in Shakespeare, Chekhov, Ibsen, and Brecht, often with success; but I believe they will be remembered by the performances I have listed, and by others of the same sort. There used to be a whole school of plays devoted to the theme of a charming lady, approaching the change of life, who falls in love with her daughter's husband: the leading actress and minor details of the story might change, but the central situation (one of the most shamelessly embarrassing ever conceived) had the rigidity of a classical convention.

During the 1950s, this type of matinée play became scarcer as a result of the Royal Court 'renaissance'. The newer dramatists – John Osborne and Arnold Wesker – had found new ways of being embarrassing; the old one had lost some of its potency through repetition (though it sometimes reappeared in a slightly altered guise, i.e. Peter Schaffer's *Five Finger Exercise*). *Look Back in Anger* exploits the vein quite brazenly with the famous 'bears and squirrels' scene. Has anyone watched this without squirming? And doesn't Osborne *mean* us to squirm? There is an equally embarrassing 'curtain' in *The Entertainer*, when Archie Rice hears that his son has been killed at Suez and, in a cracked voice, breaks into a blues song: a technical challenge which Sir Laurence Olivier, most embarrassing of great actors, was able to meet.

Wesker's plays are rooted so deeply in the concept of embarrassment that it is difficult to tell which of his effects are intentional. I suspect that he intends us to be embarrassed by his characters' humiliations (the incontinent father in *Chicken Soup with Barley*, the idealistic Socialist caught stealing firewood by an upper-class landlord in *I'm Talking About Jerusalem*) but not by their triumphs: Beatie's speech at the end of *Roots*, the barrack-room folk songs in *Chips with Everything*. Yet the triumphs are the more embarrassing (it is more embarrassing to witness elation than shame) and are therefore more theatrically effective. Perhaps the greatest achievement in the modern English theatre has been Joan Littlewood's, who found a way of exploiting embarrassment at both levels: the precarious ad-libbing of her company inducing the embarrassment of threatened disaster, that complicity with the audience of which Judy Garland is the greatest exponent; and the mixture of bawdiness with sentimentality in her most famous productions establishing the basic embarrassment of middlebrow success.

Joan Littlewood has been involved in that indignant movement against censorship which seems to be a permanent preoccupation with theatrical people. The aim has been to get four-letter words pronounced, and such themes as incest and homosexuality discussed, on the stage; for years and years the middlebrow critics have been doggedly poking fun at the Lord Chamberlain in an attempt to suggest that they are taking part in a crusade. The desirability of these once-forbidden words and subjects can only lie in their embarrassment-value – which, unfortunately, diminishes almost as soon as the ban on them is lifted (although I would not go so far as to say that it ever altogether disappears).

It looks now as if the battle with censorship has been decisively won by such dedicated directors as Peter Brook and Peter Hall. In the face of obliging protest from philistine quarters, they have discovered the 'theatre of cruelty' which conveniently provides an opportunity for combining deliberate embarrassment with culture. This Continental theatre of cruelty (Weiss, Genet, etc.) has its middlebrow British counterpart, of which Joe Orton is a successful example. Here such fashionable themes as physical violence and sexual perversion are placed against a vaguely lower-middle-class background and treated with a mannered facility recalling the work of Enid Bagnold, or even of Hugh and Margaret Williams.

It must be admitted that in the American theatre embarrassment has been carried even further than here. Tennessee Williams has probably created more embarrassment-figures than any other dramatist: impotent athletes, potty mothers, fey cripples, genteel nymphomaniacs, sex-starved spinsters, and a procession of beautiful young men to be seduced, castrated, eaten. Arthur Miller's early study in humiliation, *Death of a Salesman*, provided an orgy of embarrassment, and his later, autobiographical play, *After the Fall*, seems to have been an *embarras d'embarras*, even provoking some spectators to *admit* that they were embarrassed by it (this is rare, for audiences are as shy about confessing to embarrassment as they are reluctant to appear shocked – and, indeed, the emotions are connected). Perhaps the greatest ever embarrassment-success in the American theatre has been *Who's Afraid of Virginia Woolf?* Here Edward Albee had the daringly simple idea of writing a play about two people solely and openly motivated by the desire to embarrass each other in front of two others whose only characteristic is their extreme embarrassability: the scheme has a hermetic perfection – embarrassment biting its own tail, as it were – which makes the presence of an audience almost redundant. To feel unnecessary, actually *de trop*, is as embarrassing for an audience as its opposite, which is to feel that the performers are pathetically dependent on the spectators' goodwill, are in a sense on trial for their lives.

Neither of these alternatives has anything to do with art: and yet artists have written for the theatre. Chekhov, for example, has written *about* embarrassment – indeed, his plays consist of a subtly orchestrated series of embarrassments, major and minor, to which his characters react with varying degrees of sensibility: but they are not intended to embarrass the spectators. (When they do, it is because they are inadequately performed.) Samuel Beckett is another dramatist who has approached the theme of embarrassment with complete artistic integrity. Krapp, Winnie in *Happy Days*, the trio in *Play*, among other Beckett characters, expose our most secret thoughts, the repetitions and obsessions of the solitary mind as it is about to break loose from the moorings of social convention: these are the mad mutters we should be most embarrassed to reveal or to overhear. Beckett is so aware of the embarrassment inherent in theatrical production that his work for the stage makes provision for this, referring to it openly and stepping it up to a fever pitch where it ceases to embarrass. Winnie in her sandpit is a deliberate *reductio ad absurdum* of the tradition of the *tour de force*, from Sarah Bernhardt as an old lady with a wooden leg playing Hamlet, through Ruth Draper in her celebrated monologues talking insanely to herself on an unequivocally empty stage, elaborately dodging invisible furniture, to Olivier blacked up as a never-never nigger in *Othello*. Because Chekhov and Beckett are great writers who happen to have written

7

plays, rather than 'great playwrights', they can evoke a deeper response in an audience than the customary theatrical embarrassment. Both have given detailed instructions as to how their plays should be performed, and both have implied that actors are a necessary evil.

For it is the fact of *performance* which inevitably introduces the probability of embarrassment. There is nothing embarrassing about reading a play by Shakespeare, only about seeing it acted. It may be that the highly stylised dramatic forms developed in China and Japan achieve a classicism where embarrassment is transcended. And perhaps it was this transcendence which Stanislavsky on the one hand, with his theory of subjective identification, and Brecht on the other, with his 'alienation' technique, were attempting to match. (If so, the results have been ironic, for both methods have only increased the opportunities for elaborate displays of embarrassment.) But on the whole the Western theatre has accepted embarrassment as an inescapable end, and instead of trying to avoid it has cunningly exploited it. Playwrights devise situations, actors evolve mannerisms, calculated to induce that emotion and none other; and as this intense form of it is peculiar to the circumstances of theatrical performance, it has been tacitly recognised, and is indeed valued, as the highest response to dramatic art.

1964

Dietrich: Act of Faith

A VISIT TO THE QUEEN'S THEATRE — WHERE MARLENE
Dietrich's season has been extended one more week – can
be interpreted as an act of religious observance. These personal
appearances are solemn occasions where audiences seek a sanc-
tified outlet for hysteria combined with the satisfactory sensation of fulfilling a duty. For the performance itself, with its
liturgical overtones, is monotonous and even boring; it is not
intended to entertain, but rather to inspire awe. Just as, in early
Christian times, idolatry of local fertility goddesses was subtly
adapted to worship of the Virgin Mary, so the object of this
ancient cult retains some of the attributes of her first incarnation
as a Kurfürstendamm Venus: the husky, suggestive whisper;
the proud, yet stealthy walk; the blonde bob; the pink, transparent shimmer of her robe. These have now been stylised to
a point where memory of their original associations becomes
confused and (like a phallic symbol doing duty as an altar) they
convey such abstract qualities as courage, dignity, grace and
condescension rather than physical attraction.

The divinity has passed through many phases since her
miraculous birth as Lola-Lola in *The Blue Angel*. An unreliable
apocrypha has accumulated about her early life and how she
got this part: her own, presumably authentic version, is given
as an introduction to 'You're the Cream in My Coffee'. But
revivals of *The Blue Angel* definitely establish the historical facts
that she was at that time plumply pretty without being beautiful
and that she sang in a voice lighter and higher than it later
became. Not particularly exotic by European standards, she
must have seemed so to Hollywood when she moved there in
1930, and Josef von Sternberg cleverly emphasised this aspect in
the films which followed. Together, they created the exquisite,
equivocal creature – one of the cinema's greatest glories – who
moved languidly through such vehicles as *Morocco, Dishonoured,*

Shanghai Express and *The Devil is a Woman*. The word 'glamour' – till then a publicity man's cliché – suddenly made sense. Upholstered in furs, feathers and jewels rare and extravagant enough to satisfy Des Esseintes, she would occasionally change into top hat, starched shirt, white tie and tails. Her ideal partner was Gary Cooper, whose physical elegance perfectly complemented hers. In *Morocco*, her first American film, these glossy narcissi suggested a sexual sophistication beside which Pussy Galore looks like Joan Hunter Dunn. I remember her throwing a rose to Cooper – a lanky *légionnaire* – who coquettishly puts it behind his ear; and a scene in which he tries on Dietrich's top hat and becomes engrossed in his own reflection.

Abandoned by Sternberg, her image grew more imprecise until 1939 when, as Frenchy in *Destry Rides Again*, she allowed it to be exaggerated and even slightly guyed to please a public that had grown self-conscious and suspicious about glamour. This highly successful film was in fact the start of her decadence, a dark age of pagan fetishism during which she became the deity and main inspiration of female impersonators. It was succeeded by the present era, which finds her canonised as the patron saint of pure show-business professionalism.

To get the point of this, a great deal of faith is necessary. The faithful are required (and happily consent) to overlook some obvious difficulties: the fact, for example, that she can't really sing and therefore makes every song sound the same. Her own traditional repertoire (the sluggishly erotic 'Falling in Love Again', the embarrassingly saucy 'They Call Me Naughty Lola', the imperious 'See What the Boys in the Back Room Will Have') is distinguishable only because of its extreme familiarity from 'a song I have brought back from Israel' or ballads first sung by Tauber, Trenet, Piaf. In every case, the deep voice and slow delivery, punctuated by not very pregnant pauses, suggest an EP record played at LP speed.

Audiences are always, and rather perversely, impressed by performers who do as little as possible; they dearly love a *diseuse*. The assumption is that a great deal has been held in reserve which they are somehow unworthy of being shown. Dietrich treats her audience with a brilliantly judged combination of love and contempt. Her dazzling apparition in the flesh is sufficient proof of her love; these privileged spectators have been vouchsafed a glimpse of the godhead. But, once *on* the stage, she does the minimum. Her hieratic gestures are limited and essentially meaningless; in fact she is most effective when she remains completely still, as in 'Where Have All the Flowers Gone?' With a gay, fast number like 'My Blue Heaven', she merely extends her arms sideways at shoulder-level, points her forefingers and revolves them in time to the beat. This allows her otherwise to ignore the rhythm of the song while leading her audience to believe that they are witnessing the art which conceals art. They find this more flattering (because less obviously enjoyable) than hearing the tune sung properly, and the trick works; for theatre audiences share a streak of masochism with religious congregations. As in church, no jokes are allowed; although one is permitted to laugh at utterly humourless references to incidents in Dietrich's career – a social, empty laugh, conveying recognition and encouragement, which genuine funniness would stifle. These mock-modest sallies, like the harmless blasphemy of a jolly priest, are a variation on reverence.

The theatre is a place where it is difficult enough to work one illusion: Dietrich undertakes two. The first, a variation on the old mirror trick, is purely physical. Sustained by clothes, make-up, lighting and confidence, she looks beautiful, neither young nor old. The second is more ambitious and more subtle. Fixing us with her sad and serious gaze, she hypnotises us into seeing her as holy, untouchable – who would dare to criticise a sacred rite? What she does is neither difficult nor diverting, but the fact that she does it at all fills the onlookers with wonder. She is helped, of course, by her fame and her past, and also by the sheer silliness of show-business snobbery. It takes two to make a conjuring trick: the illusionist's sleight of hand and the stooge's desire to be deceived. To these necessary elements (her own technical competence and her audience's sentimentality) Marlene Dietrich adds a third – the mysterious force of her belief in her own magic. Those who find themselves unable to share this belief tend to blame themselves rather than her.

At the climax of her first-night triumph, a procession of usherettes marched across the stage bearing bouquets: she kissed them all. Not content with this vicarious contact, individual members of the audience, crazed by ecstasy, surged forward to place flowers at her feet. There was nothing here of the automatic abandon of Beatlemania: this was a reverent exaltation, hallowed by time and strengthened by the basic irrationality of the miracle it celebrates.

1964

COMEBACK

O N A STAIRCASE WALL DEEP INSIDE THE AUDITORIUM OF THE London Palladium there hangs a plaque in memory of 'the incomparable Judy Garland'. A sober quote from the *Daily Telegraph* is inscribed beneath a photograph of the star, with the dates of her birth and death and her appearances at this particular theatre. It was here, in 1950, when it looked as if her career on the screen was over, that she made her first historic comeback. Fat and frightened, bemused by the frantic fans whom she thought had forgotten her, she tripped and fell on the stage on opening night, then staggered to her feet and began to sing. It was then that she captured that special audience over whom she was to retain a mystic hold for the rest of her life, and even beyond it – an audience composed partly of loyal, if slightly hysterical homosexuals, and partly of the Palladium's regular patrons, that brashly hedonist branch of the mercantile bourgeoisie who are also seasoned epicures of true show-business quality. Her success in London gave her the confidence to appear the following year at the Palace in New York, where the legend of 'Judy live' began: the other, Hollywood, legend had started in 1937, when she was fourteen. Her last Palladium concert was in 1965, four years before her death, when she shared the bill with her daughter, Liza Minnelli. As if by magic, all seats were sold out before the event had been advertised. Liza revealed herself as an attractive, competent entertainer, with a singing style at that time influenced by Barbra Streisand. Judy seemed at moments to be showing more than her usual disregard of her public; she forgot her words and her voice was often uncertain. But she sang 'Smile' as it had never been sung before, and when she joined Liza in an overwhelming version of 'Chicago' the holders of the most extortionately expensive black-market tickets knew that they had got their money's worth.

Exactly four weeks ago, on Friday, 11 May, tickets for Liza

Minnelli's midnight matinee were changing hands outside the Palladium for £50 each. I got into conversation with a party of disgruntled American homosexuals who had crossed the Atlantic specially for the occasion but could not afford that price. They told me on no account to miss Jim Bailey, who was making his English debut at this theatre on Sunday, 27 May, for a single concert. 'He does an impersonation of Judy that's so like her it's *unreal*.' The celebrities arrived: Barbara Windsor, Bianca Jagger, Marlene Dietrich with her grandson. But the anonymous bulk of the audience seemed to me the same as in 1950 and in 1965. Liza, now herself a superstar, was no longer at all like Streisand. She made no mention of her mother, or of her awe at finding herself back at the Palladium. Her pleasant, inventive and versatile performance owed nothing to sentimental nostalgia and everything to her own appealing personality – a disciplined gaucheness, a bright pathos, a cleverly concealed resilience which had made her an almost perfect Sally Bowles. At one point the microphone broke down: Judy would have turned the incident into a tragi-comedy, but Liza hid her momentary embarrassment at this minor mishap behind a smooth professionalism. The show must go on and it did. While the glamour of Judy's act derived from the fascinating fear of failure, Liza's is solidly based in the assurance of success. Unusually talented, she is no more than normally vulnerable. I think the fans were relieved: who could bear to go through all that exquisite agony again? But relief may have been, as it often is, tinged with a teasing disappointment.

Perhaps it was this ambivalent reaction that brought me and (as it seemed) an identical audience back to the Palladium for Jim Bailey's show. Were we impelled by a death wish, or in search of an intimation of immortality? Judy's fans are all initiates in a mystery: they understand that entertainment can partake of a sacramental quality. Liza's brilliance had established a consoling sense of continuity for them, but the experience had stopped short of the miraculous. Tangible reincarnation had not yet occurred. The pale, nervous, quarrelsome hairdressers and the furred, eager ladies from Golders Green had come to the Palladium tonight as to a spiritualist seance. Only the phenomenal would satisfy them.

Bailey started with a stunning imitation of Barbra Streisand: clearly he was outstandingly gifted as a mimic and a parodist. Subtle, accurate observation gave us the next best thing to Streisand herself; but the love was lacking that might have brought about a total identification. A mediocre comedian followed: we tolerated him, for we knew that Jim needed plenty of time in which to effect his transformation into Judy. Apart from the technical complexities of make-up and dress necessary to achieve a physical resemblance, he must surely require, like any Method actor, a period of repose in which to bring about an internal metamorphosis. After the interval, there came a solemn announcement: 'Mr Jim Bailey will now offer his tribute to the immortal Miss Judy Garland.' The long overture began – that familiar, tantalising medley of 'Over the Rainbow', 'The Trolley Song' and 'The Man That Got Away' in which again and again a portentously loud *legato* seems to herald an entrance which does not take place, protracting the suspense to a point nearly unbearable for the audience who can sense a nameless terror in the wings. Then, at an unexpected moment, an unseen hand pushed her on stage: the hesitant sidling steps, the ironic humble bows, the confident grab of the microphone and the insolent sling of the flex over one shoulder, suddenly a moment of naked fear, now the purposeful prowl and at last a triumphant song: 'What a *day* this has been . . . !' The crowd sighed, relaxed, lowered their opera-glasses. It was going to be all right.

Jim Bailey sang all of Judy Garland's most famous numbers exactly as she would have done herself, with 'Swanee' as an induced request and 'A Foggy Day in London Town' in honour of the venue. He managed a costume change, preceded by a meandering, uneasily informal chat with the orchestra which nearly got bogged down in laborious jokes about Grace Kelly (who won an Oscar in the year Judy had earned it with *A Star is Born*). He sat on the floor in a single spotlight and sang 'Over the Rainbow'. 'Immortal' was right: Judy was back at the Palladium. Why had one doubted? Of course, quite simply, she was the best ever.

1973

P. J. PROBY

'I FEEL KIND OF BLUE TODAY,' SAID P. J. PROBY. 'BLUE AND hungover. I spent last night drinking with a friend of mine. He was very depressed and talking about suicide. I cheered him up and depressed myself! He was worried that he wasn't a *star*, that his *marriage* was unhappy, all that. Everyone's problems are so alike, his reminded me of the ones I'd only just got over.'

Proby was dressed from head to foot in baby blue. 'I don't do any two-tone bullshit,' he said. 'Everything's the same with me – coat, pants, shoes and the bow in my hair. This is the last of the goddam suits – the fans have torn all the others to bits. I'll have to go over to France for some more. It's a special stretched velvet you can only get over there – there's no demand for it in England. These pants are so damned tight, it's unreal. But they're made for the stage – you can do *anything* in them. See this loose jacket? Hides my beer belly!' He took a noisy swig of Scotch, camouflaged in a Coca-Cola bottle. Proby is supposed not to drink spirits, which might harm his voice. 'But wine drives you out of your mind! I tell you, I'm losing my mind on wine . . .'

Proby is a tough-looking Texan of twenty-seven, six feet tall, with a deep, fruity speaking-voice. On the stage he adopts effeminate mannerisms and blatantly sexual gestures which have little to do with his personality in real life. His long hair and velvet suit were therefore more disconcerting off the stage, where they seemed pointless and almost embarrassing, as if he had mistakenly gone out of doors in his pyjamas.

'Shape of my head look okay?' he asked as he posed for some photographs. 'Be sure you blot out my double chin when my face is at this angle. Anything under *here*' (tapping chin) 'I want out of that picture. Why, even Prince Philip would look like an idiot if you gave him a double chin. I guess you want me kind

16

of lackadaisical in this one? I got two profiles, you know, one good and one bad. I'm quite a different person one side of my face to the other. This is my worst side, so take that goddam hump out of my nose if you can, with shadow or something. Give me an *aquiline* nose. Want me to wear my bracelet? A girl just gave me this. It's sterling silver. I told her, I prefer gold.' He examined it. 'Christ, I believe it's *brass!*'

Proby is unusually old for a pop star. After an undistinguished career in American show business, he came to England last year where his extravagant appearance and bizarre, suggestive style of singing soon became popular with a very young audience. Increasing complaints from adults, however, have recently limited his appearances. 'But I've got an Australian tour coming up in August. And before that I go back to Los Angeles for three TV shows.

'My whole act is made up from different girls I've been with. I took the walk from a girl in Hollywood, the body movements from a dancer in *The Ed Sullivan Show*, and the pout from Chrissie Shrimpton. Now I see on TV that Tom Jones is copying the pouting bit. But I don't think that it will work with him, because when he pouts he looks like a basset hound.

'The Tom Jones bow was my own idea. I've always lived in a fantasy world, so I decided to wear my hair in a ponytail, like they did in the olden times. I've learned a lot about hair. Every man had long hair till the First World War – short hair only came in for the troops, for hygienic reasons. But this year I'm going to cut it all off and go for the adult market. I want to move from the *hysteria* stage to the *applause* stage, and you only get hysteria from the kids. I'm hoping to star in a movie, too – *The Greatest Story Never Told*. About a pop star who goes off his head and believes he's Jesus Christ. Then I want to make a whole series playing a sort of a Bond-type character. That's what I want – to play *characters*. I've been playing P. J. Proby so long I'm getting tired of myself.

'The kids will forgive me, when I cut off my hair. It will be done in such a way that they won't mind. If you're *truthful* with the fans, they'll take anything, even if it's bullshit. I tell them some tall Texan story and they know I'm not serious. But it's got to be *truthful* bullshit.

'That's what I deal in – raw truth. In England they don't like the raw truth. Know what I think when some lady in Hereford or somewhere says I'm disgusting and obscene? I pity her. I just think: "You frigging fool." What would have happened if Elvis ever came to England? Same as happened with me. Banned all over the place so he'd have to work in crummy ballrooms where they decorate the stage with toilet paper. I come over here and I do *more* than the English boys, I go further. They don't trust foreigners so they make me feel like a nigger must feel in Alabama. They can't take the *raw truth*.'

Cars were thickly parked outside the California Ballroom, a bright, gimcrack building perched on a windy hill near Dunstable. On the evening of Proby's appearance there, it was cynically supervised by a cordon of police. A nearby bungalow – home of the Ballroom's manageress, Mrs King – served as the pop star's dressing room. He slouched on a chair in the daintily decorated sitting room, surrounded by statuettes of crinolined ladies, his hair in metal grips sticking out all round his head like Medusa's. Barry, his personal assistant, was engaged on the long and complicated ceremony of Proby's coiffure – an intricate ritual of back-combing and pinning, involving a tool-kit as extensive as a garage mechanic's. An odd little man, with spectacles mended by Elastoplast and a look of Peter Lorre, sat on a sofa reading a paperback on vampires: Bongo Wolf, Proby's best friend. A dark girl, Leslie, was paying vague attention to a budgie in a cage. Terry, Proby's bodyguard, stood stiff in a corner. The pop star held forth.

'I left Houston when I was seventeen because there was no show business there. Had to choose between two places – New York and Hollywood. I chose wrong. I'd been singing with Tommy Sands at the Hitching Post in Houston, and he was dating my sister, so I followed Tommy to Hollywood. Now in New York there is competition, maybe 200 people after the same job, but if you're talented you have a chance of getting it. In Hollywood there's a clique – if you're not in the clique, you don't work. For years I bashed my ass against a brick wall. You only make it if you stick it out and don't give up. Some of the ones who leave are even more talented than you are. But you're *there*. I worked in B movies of the hot-rod era, things like *Dragstrip*. And I did the demos for Elvis movies. I'd record all the numbers sounding just like Elvis, so that when he got through acting he could come and learn the songs straight off my demos. I've known Elvis since I was fourteen – he used to go with my sister. But Elvis won't talk to me now. While he was in the army I became quite involved with one of his girlfriends, is the reason. Though I hear that since I've made it over here in Britain, Elvis wants to have me round to the house again. What he minded was his girl being balled by a nobody. Funny thing, you really get to know a guy when you date his girl. Mick Jagger has forbidden all of the Stones to speak to me because I went out with Chrissie Shrimpton. But all she did was talk of Mick all the time. Mick's a very sensitive kid. I really got to know the inside of that boy, but I guess he'll never know it.'

Jimmy Henny, Proby's road manager, entered the room: a nervous man with a manner at the same time distracted and brash. He fussily told Proby that he was due on stage. After a disapproving pause, Proby cleared his throat and noisily spat several yards beyond the electric fire and straight into the grate. He hadn't seen Henny since their return from Denmark, when there had been a mix-up at London Airport – the road manager had failed to lay on a car and the fans had got out of control. 'Next time I won't get off the ramp till there's a car to meet me like there is with the Beatles and the Stones. Understand?' Henny began to defend himself, rather hysterically, but the animosity in the room was too strong, and he left it.

'But Denmark was unreal,' said Proby. 'No pop star ever had such an ovation. Here it's the girls who surge forward just to touch me, but there it was the boys rushed on to the stage to shake my hand. I didn't get it at first – I thought they were hostile, and began punching them! The ones at the back would make themselves stiff, like arrows, and be passed forward over the heads of the others. We had a ball in Denmark, didn't we, Bongo?'

'Yeah,' said Bongo. 'I brought back some artistic mementoes.' He produced a packet of nude photographs.

Leslie, who has a reputation for being psychic, suddenly looked at Barry and said: 'I get Ethel. Do you know an Ethel?' He shook his head. 'You will,' said Leslie.

The metal pins were now out of Proby's hair and fastened to Barry's jacket. As he manipulated the stiff black mass, Barry clicked his tongue in wonder: 'Leslie's fantastic. She told me I'd meet a lovely blonde girl in Denmark, and I did. The other day she got through to my dead Gran who told her something about a blue and green sweater. It meant nothing to me. So I rang my mother, and she said yes, your Gran *did* knit you a blue and green sweater when you were small.'

'Unreal,' said Proby. 'Bongo's a warlock, aren't you, Bongo?' He saw that Bongo was stroking Mrs King's cat, which had jumped on to his lap. Proby startled the room by suddenly bellowing: 'Leave that cat alone!' Then, softer but still sternly: 'You frighten animals. You touch them too hard.'

Proby explained about Bongo. 'That's not his real name. His real name is Donald Grollman, but he loves to play the bongos and he's interested in werewolves, so we call him Bongo Wolf. We've been buddies five years now. Bongo seems to be mentally deranged but that isn't true and he's the kindest guy in the world. Although he's thirty-three years of age he still lives with his parents in Hollywood. My father was rich and when I first came to Hollywood I kept a lot of people, but after he cut me off I went round all these former friends asking for handouts and none were giving any. Except Bongo. When my wife and I were nearly starving, he'd throw us trays of frozen TV dinners out the window, we'd grab 'em up and run off home. I swore then that if I ever made it I'd show Bongo the world, and that's what I'm doing. Something he'd never be able to do without me. I may seem to be cruel to him sometimes, but it's for his own good – for his health.'

'Maybe,' said Bongo. 'But I wish you and the boys would lay off teasing me, making out like I'm a faggot. It's a joke, but it gets boring.'

Henny returned, more agitated than ever. Proby was now *very* overdue. But he wouldn't be hurried – 'Let them wait.' At last Barry produced, and carefully folded, a white satin coat with the Texas flag on it in red and blue. 'I wear this at the end of my act,' said Proby. 'When my trousers split.' Henny winced. Bongo said: 'You've *got* to be joking!'

Protected by his entourage, Proby was swiftly smuggled across a dark courtyard to the ballroom, which was now unhealthily full of impatient fans. Henny approached a police officer at the door. 'I'm P. J. Proby's manager,' he announced, and held out his hand. Surprisedly shaking it, the policeman replied: 'Well, good luck to you then. I'm Inspector Lambert – *his* manager' – and pointed to another policeman, with an irony which Henny missed.

The stage was guarded by an impressive group of chuckers-out. Proby crouched in the wings. He took a last, long pull at the Coca-Cola bottle and asked for a mirror. A panic-stricken whisper was repeated: 'Is there a mirror in the office?' Eventually a small powder compact was produced and urgently passed down the line of policemen and chuckers-out. 'Jesus Christ, I'm getting a beard under my eyes,' said Proby; then, extending his arms in an ineffably camp gesture, he tripped daintily on to the stage. The roars of the audience drowned his theme song, 'Somewhere'.

Proby claims that if one fan in the audience stops screaming, he hears it and acts accordingly. His performance takes forty-five minutes, but can be much longer if he ad-libs: it depends on the audience reaction. On this occasion, there was a steady roar – stimulated less by his voice and the music, which could hardly be heard, than by his voluptuous massaging of his buttocks and groin, his queenly gestures and mincing gait. The blue velvet, dangerously stretched, gleamed in the spotlight. 'Am I clean?' he called out. 'Don't you want to touch me? Am I clean?' 'Yes! Yes!' they yelled back, and arms stretched out to him – but a line of bodyguards in front of the stage prevented any physical contact. Mrs King had been over-cautious in protecting her ballroom – physical contact is the *point* of Proby's act. Stinging drops of sweat flew from his body to land on the grim faces of the guards below, punishing them with temporary blindness.

*

After the show, his uniform limp and stained with sweat, Proby lay for a while unconscious in Mrs King's bungalow. 'He could get fabulous crumpet at some of these concerts,' said Barry. 'See all those birds go wild? But he always passes out. The strain is terrible.'

When he came to, Proby said that the performance had been a disaster. 'No audience participation. That line of chuckers-out stopped the fans from getting anywhere near me. That's the last time I work in a ballroom. From now on it's genuine *concerts*, like in Denmark, or I don't work.' He began to change into street clothes: black velvet trousers, open white shirt, white sweater, white socks, black buckled shoes. His hair was allowed to hang loose in a long dark bob, between which his jutting, grinning, handsome features had a fleeting look of Mary McCarthy.

Proby and his entourage were sedately conducted back to London in a chauffeur-driven Rolls. The car was delayed in a traffic block beside a Post Office van, driven by a woman in a postman's uniform. Proby, who had been silent, shook his head and spoke in rich, elegiac tones: 'It's just terrible to see a woman working like a man, and dressing like a man, and looking like a man, and everything. There's no excuse for it.'

Proby's house in Chelsea is filled with firearms of every size: the drawing-room walls are hung with antlers. A pretty girl was waiting there; she was introduced as Sarah, and poured out drinks. 'All these cannons fire,' he said. 'Most of these objects I owe on still. Can't afford the Portobello Road at the moment. You like good music, don't you? I'll play you my new LP. This is not commercial, it's the classics. Standards from shows like *Carousel* and *Oklahoma*. You see, I'm old enough to remember the forties singers – Sinatra, Dick Haymes. These younger boys were only exposed to the fifties and rock 'n' roll, so they don't have any standards. Just listen to this. When all the teenage shit is over, I'll have this to fall back on.' A slow, syrupy version of 'If I Loved You' was listened to in reverent silence. 'I wish we had mission bells there, goddam it,' Proby muttered at the end.

A basset hound lumbered into the room: Mister President, a

gift from the President of the P. J. Proby fan club. 'I'm crazy about animals. I have a cat too, called Marmaduke. And Japanese goldfish – they're so beautiful! I love to walk in the park and watch people and their dogs. Have you ever noticed how people get to look like their pets? Dachshunds – they're so individual, it's unreal. Trotting on, ignoring their masters, like they said "I think I'll just go take a walk by myself". One thing I have to have, a Saint Bernard. Maybe when Mister President is a little older, so he won't get jealous.'

Mister President jumped on to the drawing-room sofa. After a shocked pause, Proby bellowed at Sarah: 'GET HIM OFF!' The dog jumped down, alarmed, and Sarah began: 'I thought . . . ' 'Don't think!' Proby shouted. 'Act!'

The telephone rang, barely audible above Proby's singing on the gramophone. Sarah went to answer it. 'If it's a fan, hang up. I'm not interested. Tell her if she comes round I'll punch the hell out of her. Women come round here when *I* want them.' Sarah hung up. Proby patted her face. 'She'd be all right if she wasn't so fat,' he said. 'Good little cheekbones and nose, but all round here will have to go.'

'That's puppy fat,' said Sarah. 'I'm not eighteen yet, am I?'

'My type is the petite type,' Proby went on. 'I don't mean I couldn't ball Sophia Loren, but in the perspective of like marriage, and living with a woman all your life, I don't like them too big. Marriage! I'm kind of cynical about marriage. I divorced my wife for one reason – cheating. I never cheated on her till she implanted in my mind the idea that she was cheating on me. So I left for England a year ago and haven't seen her since. One good thing, we didn't have any kids. I've several illegitimate ones, and if I don't have any real ones, some day when I'm very old I might leave something to the ones I have. But only if I don't have any real ones. If my wife had had children, and she'd got custody of them after the divorce, I'd have shot her. Then she'd be dead, I'd go to the electric chair, and they'd be put in military school which wouldn't do any harm. I was made a ward of court myself at twelve, and had a military upbringing, and I'm in favour of the discipline. All I've done in the world I owe to that military discipline.'

The entourage began to drift away. 'I think I'll go to the Ad

Lib tonight,' said Proby. 'I don't feel like sitting around alone.'

'But you're not alone,' said Sarah.

'Yes, I am too alone,' said the pop star. 'When you're dealing with yourself, you're alone.'

1965

THE EMBARRASSMENT OF
BEING EAMONN

LEADING FIGURES IN THE THEATRE, CINEMA AND POPULAR
music are known as stars, but their equivalents on television
are referred to as personalities. A star, we are told, is larger
than life: some recognisable human trait is exaggerated by a
single performer, whose appeal combines the familiar with the
fantastic. But in the homespun medium of television, this rule
is reversed: a personality, to be really successful, must lack not
only star quality, but also noticeable personality. Hence that
curious phenomenon of modern show business – the man who
seems somehow smaller than life, provocative in his nullity,
extraordinary only in his dogged exploitation of the ordinary.
Hence Eamonn Andrews, one of the most popular and highly
paid television personalities for well over a decade.

In a fortnight *The Eamonn Andrews Show* returns to the air
after a summer recess. This will be the 118th programme, and
the first in its fourth year. 'Can *you* understand the secret of his
success?' said the director, Ronald Fouracre. 'I can't. He's only
interested in his family and in golf.'

Eamonn himself seems equally bewildered (which may be
part of the secret). 'Who can define a rose? It's too simple and
too complicated. But if any theme does emerge from the letters
fans write me, it's that I'm one of them. I'm nothing special or
remote, just a viewer who by accident happens to find himself
on the other side of the television cameras.'

Accident is a key word here. His most famous programmes
have been constructed round the simultaneous threat and
promise of unrehearsed disaster. Eamonn's apprehensive expression alerts viewers to the continual danger of overwhelming
embarrassment. Traumatically, once a week he lives out their
social nightmares: an inexperienced host, accidentally trapped

in the public eye while he fails to cope with the emergencies created by hysterical, drunken, abusive, or just plain boring guests.

'I really went into show business by accident. My predilection was towards writing. I used to be very fond of thrillers – Sapper, Peter Cheyney, Ian Fleming, Mickey Spillane. I'd love to write one and act in it – but I don't have much time now for writing.'

In 1941 he did write and act in a drama called *The Moon is Black*, which was performed without success in Dublin. It was about a tubercular husband who decides to murder his wife, in order to preserve her beauty. He does so, not realising that she is already dead – and is then tormented by guilt without knowing the truth. Eamonn has also written an autobiography, *This is My Life*, published in 1963. This contains the modest statement: 'It's a constant source of amazement to me that what I do is something that earns me a living. What exactly do I do? Be myself, I think that's the answer.'

But what exactly is that? Well, he was born nearly forty-five years ago, the son of a Dublin carpenter, and educated by the Irish Christian Brothers. A former middleweight All-Ireland Amateur Junior Boxing Champion, he was a sports broadcaster for Radio Eireann from 1941 to 1950, and then came to London and the BBC. In 1951 he married and made his first television appearance. Sport inevitably led to show business and it was the success of *What's My Line?* in 1953 which established him as a 'personality' – along with such legendary figures of the fifties as Gilbert Harding and the Ladies Barnett and Boyle. Two years later, the tear-jerking *This is Your Life* consolidated his popularity.

From 1960 to 1966 he was Chairman of Irish Television. He has numerous business interests and is a director of Arbiter & Weston – a firm controlling gambling clubs, bingo halls and music companies. In 1964 the Catholic Church made him a Knight of St Gregory and he left the BBC for ABC television, which is said to pay him between £40,000 and £50,000 a year. He is six feet tall – slow, rather sentimental and very businesslike. A colleague said of him: 'It's fascinating the way Eamonn uses time. He realises it's money. But he never seems hurried.' Another suggested: 'It's just because he *is* so negative that the show sometimes works. The guests feel they must make an effort to help him – while with somebody smarter, like David Frost, they'd be inhibited.'

'It's the Art of the Possible,' said Eamonn about his pro- gramme. 'Where else would you find Gypsy Rose Lee and Ted Hill together? Or Manny Shinwell talking to Lulu? I've always loved good conversation.

'What talkers from history would I choose for my ideal show? Well, an Irishman – I'd want Shaw but I suspect I'd choose Wilde. Cleopatra if she spoke English. Somebody like Cassius Clay out of sport who would be extrovert. Toscanini. And some unknown. I love finding unknown talkers.

'But our emphasis is inevitably on show-business people. They're used to the medium, they're prepared to come along, people know them. And we have more men than women, because men are more acceptable. Women are either too demure – they think it's unladylike to jump in, and if you force them they're stuck out on a limb. Or they jump in themselves, and offend the public.

'Very few people refuse to be on the show – and then it's usually because they *can't*, owing to contractual arrangements. The ones who clamour to be on it are the ones we don't want. It gives actors excellent exposure.

'Kenneth Williams got *International Cabaret* – he'd never done any stand-up stuff before. Dora Bryan got *Hello Dolly!* – Mary Martin was watching, she said, "There's your Dolly." And what about Arthur Tracy? He got a theatre contract just from sitting in the audience!

'The show should be open-ended. But there's this terrible problem about how many hours each company is allowed. It's probably decided by some little civil servant in some obscure office. Every week the guests are surprised when it's over. Americans can never understand it – "But Baby, I just said Hello!" And it doesn't seem logical to the viewers – why end there? So I get the blame. Ideally, I'd love an extra twenty minutes over the forty-five. Now the show has to be pressure- cooked, and sometimes the discipline of the clock makes a better programme. But it can take time to relax people, to reassure them without patronising them. Sometimes I ache inside me when I see that time's up just as they're beginning to forget the cameras.

'Originally the show was live. Then we changed *Live from London* to *Tonight from London*, though some people still think we're saying "live". And at first I didn't meet the guests at all beforehand. I wanted to prove it was unscripted and unrehearsed. Basically I believe in being honest and sincere about these things. But the people I didn't know, especially Americans, thought I was being grand, or just bloody rude – so now I meet them for a few minutes before. I'm always terrified they'll get into a rehearsal by mistake.

'At the beginning I thought my role was just to bring them together and I shouldn't express opinions. Now I've come to the conclusion that's wrong, I should try to show my opinions more. I don't know whether I do it enough. But by asking questions, I state my position quite clearly. People accuse me of favouring RCs. But I've had Paddy Campbell on the show – and he's a bloody Orangeman! And what about Spike Milligan, screaming "Take the pill!" at me? Though you could say we've had a religious influence: the *Epilogue* ratings have gone up with ours. We have fantastic viewing figures for so late at night.'

Eamonn lives at Chiswick in a large white house called Park Nasilla. The lawn, reaching down to the river, is covered in daisies. 'The purist doesn't like them, but I think of them as stars on the grass.' The household contains his wife Grainne, their adopted children Emma and Fergal, three dogs and a bird – but apart from the bright yellow nursery, there is something curiously impersonal about Park Nasilla. The bowl of fruit on the polished dining table, the wrought-iron door, elaborate red lampshades, black cushions, decorative greenery, undistinguished oil-paintings and an abundance of table-lighters rather suggest a furnished hotel suite. No books in sight, except for an engagement diary with a few, neat entries: a reception for Apostolic Delegates at the Rembrandt Hotel, a garden party given by Beverley Nichols. ('I have no social life.') One looking-glass door leads to a cocktail cabinet; its twin leads to the den. Here, on the morning of the last Sunday in June, Eamonn was in conference with his producer, Malcolm Morris, and two researchers, Tom Brennand and Roy Bottomley.

They were discussing the final programme in the third year, after which Eamonn could join his family for their annual three months' holiday in Ireland. 'I'd like to finish off with a smile. One idea I've been playing around with – something like "Goodbye, it's our last show. Dave Allen's taking over. Since he appeared on the show he's had insomnia." But how do I develop it? Would it be funny to say "mixsomnia" or something?' Nobody answered.

The guests expected that evening were Phil Silvers, Kenneth Williams, Dahlia Lavi and Roger Moore. Considerable thought had gone into the order of their appearance. Silvers, as the star, would come on last; and Williams, as the most likely to be amusing when alone with Andrews, would be first. Moore would be brought on second, and Lavi third – 'Because she's more likely to react to Roger than to Kenny, it's a basic sexual thing.'

'Lavi can read palms,' said Morris. 'Can we get her to read Roger's?'

'I'm more concerned with the end of the show,' said Eamonn. 'I must have some sort of goodnight, with Phil Silvers rambling on . . .'

'Don't let's make too big a thing of the palmistry. We've got the knickersuit in, remember.'

'Sammy Davis is *choked* he can't do the show. Absolutely *choked*. But he had this BBC special. You don't realise the turmoil we churned up there by trying to get him. A certain gentleman who shall be nameless but is known as Tom Sloan just did his nut.'

The conference was interrupted by a clap of thunder. 'It's OK, God!' Eamonn shouted, addressing the sky. 'We're coming back in October!'

By six o'clock that evening he was seated gravely behind an office desk at Teddington Studios. An austere room, containing little else than Eamonn's supper-tray (a bowl of fruit and two bottles of milk) and a shelf of books: *Cicely* by Cicely Court-neidge, *I Remember Romano's* by Henry Kendall, *Lucky Star* by Margaret Lockwood, *Come Dance with Me* by Ninette de Valois. The Press Officer plucked moodily at the photograph of a blonde actress pasted on the door. 'We're besieged by these stickers of Yvette Mimieux. When she was on the show her manager put them up all over the bloody place.'

Eamonn was studying a series of little cards, on which scraps of information about this evening's guests had been typed. His lips moved silently as he struggled to memorise the items. The guests had been interviewed during the week by his researchers, who had then collated the material: their dread was that conversation on the show might turn towards some subject about which Eamonn had not been briefed.

'There's something about Kenneth Williams in one of the papers today,' he said. 'I need a copy at once.'

At 7.30 he went down to the studio for a brief camera rehearsal. The massive set, made of metal, and the special little green room beside it for his guests to wait in, look like a permanent fixture: but in fact they are dismantled every Monday morning until the following week.

'This is when we start to get nervous,' said Morris, while the moves and seating arrangements were vaguely run through with studio technicians standing in for the guests. The man impersonating Dahlia Lavi made a mincing entrance, which gave rise to uneasy facetiousness. Eamonn wore an air of slightly abstracted imperturbability. 'Does this chair give enough room for Miss Lavi's lower appendages?' he inquired.

After the rehearsal, Eamonn retired to his room once more while the guests began to arrive. Invited for 7.45, they were greeted at the gates by 'Security' and conducted to the Admin Room, where the researchers entertained them with drinks, sandwiches and conversation.

A great many compliments were exchanged in the Admin Room. Dahlia Lavi's dress was widely admired, and Phil Silvers said to Kenneth Williams, with emotion in his voice: 'I've *really* enjoyed you.' 'Ditto,' said Williams. Roger Moore was watching himself as the Saint on a television set.

At 8.30 the studio audience was admitted, and friends and relations accompanying the guests left the Admin Room for the studio downstairs. The guests began to talk less, to walk restlessly about the room. Then at 8.45 Eamonn appeared, and the atmosphere of false conviviality was resumed.

He spent some time in conversation with Phil Silvers, and

then abruptly left the room, followed by his production team. There was an anxious consultation in the passage. Eamonn was tense: 'I'm not going back in there!' he repeated. It emerged that Silvers had been so impressed by the recent appearance of Jerry Lewis on the show, when the art of comedy had been seriously discussed, that he intended to be equally serious tonight. 'He'll wreck it!' said Eamonn, in a panic. 'We only asked him because he's meant to be funny! Oh God!'

At last the others went back to talk to Silvers, while Eamonn descended to the make-up room. He was trembling. 'Smile, though your heart is breaking,' he sang in an unsteady Irish tenor. 'What an exit line!'

While he was being made up, he complained: 'I'm usually so calm when I come in here but now I've got the jitters. Why? I've just seen the guests, that's why!' Someone followed him in to say: 'You know that Madam would like to be called Lavee?' 'What do you mean? What are you talking about?' 'She says that's how she pronounces her name.' 'Oh, I see. I suppose Lavi sounds too like the other thing.'

The studio doors had been closed at 8.45 and the audience was now being 'warmed up' by John Benson, the announcer. 'He always tells the same jokes in the warm-up; that way you can judge how good the audience is.'

Eamonn peeped through a crack in the back of the set, and grunted. He went into the green room and poured himself a large whiskey. A Sunday paper was brought to him – but it was the wrong edition, and did not contain the quote about Kenneth Williams. This seemed to unsettle him further.

'The funny thing is,' said Eamonn, 'I'm supposed to go out in a minute and warm them up by telling them who's coming on. But I can't remember the names of the guests.' With an agonised face, he muttered: 'Lavi – I mean Lavee – Moore . . . no, I *can't* remember!'

The guests entered the green room. 'Is this the warm-up?' said Silvers, hearing tepid laughter from the audience. 'Who can follow that?' A girl brought in a tray containing make-up and Kleenex, and gave Eamonn's face a final dab. Before he went onstage, the guests called out 'Good luck!' and 'Have fun!'

'It's the grace of God, that's what it is,' he replied with an almost noble desperation.

But he had enough professional experience to exploit a crisis, and when he announced the guests he *pretended* to have forgotten their names, making the audience laugh.

At nine o'clock, the show began. It got off to a promising start with Kenneth Williams making a series of homosexual jokes. The guests remaining in the green room worked themselves up into a fever of enthusiasm. 'He's one of the brightest boys I ever met!' said Silvers. 'And he has charm, too.' Then Matt Monro sang a song. 'What a fabulous voice!' said Dahlia Lavi.

One of the researchers was having a little chat with Silvers. 'Don't say about how lovely you think London is – you know, the Garland bit. All Americans think they have to. But the public is more interested in *you* than in what you think about *them*.' 'I'll get that over quickly,' said Silvers.

But when he went on, he failed to keep his promise. He spoke for a very long time about how lovely he thought London was, and described in detail an encounter with the Queen: 'Nobody can take that away from me!' The researchers in the green room were groaning; and on the set, Eamonn had clearly lost control. 'Fair enough, fair enough,' he kept on saying meaninglessly.

Then Silvers embarked on a complicated anecdote about Frank Sinatra, Bing Crosby and the Pope, which became more and more unctuous and sentimental. A light flashed on and off in the green room: the producer signalling acute distress. 'Fair enough,' said Eamonn, looking wildly round for help. 'Who are you looking at?' said Silvers. 'At you,' Eamonn lied. Backstage, the panic grew. 'He's killing the show stone dead, and nobody can do anything about it,' said Roy Bottomley.

'There's one thing we *can* do,' said Tom Brennand solemnly. 'We've never done it before and we hoped we never would. But we could run overtime and then cut the tape.' After consultation by telephone with the control room, it was decided to take this desperate expedient.

When the show was over, Silvers left at once and Eamonn signed autographs for fans in the audience while a rather gloomy gathering assembled in the Admin Room. They had run eight minutes overtime, and the whole of the anecdote about the Pope was being cut. This had to be done quickly: it was now nearly ten o'clock, and in some areas the show went on the air at 10.45.

When Eamonn returned to the Admin Room, he poured himself another whiskey. 'It's the first time the show has ever been cut at all,' he said miserably. 'It's against all our basic principles. The whole point is we're unrehearsed, unscripted and unedited. But the Pope bit had to go. It's not that we're anti-Pope – we're just anti-bore. What was such a *crucifixion* for me was that I could have handled him. I could have handled him! But then he'd have been Sergeant Bilko, sweet and pathetic, and all the viewers would have pitied him and hated me. Oh, it was an agony.'

Then he went back to Park Nasilla to watch the agony at 11.15.

1967

THE SUB-CINEMA

CERTAIN BRANCHES OF THE BRITISH CINEMA ARE ABLE TO weather any crisis: they do not so much rise above it as sink beneath it, to a subterranean level where the storms over quotas and television competition cannot affect them. This sub-cinema consists mainly of two parallel institutions, both under ten years old: the Hammer horror and the Carry On comedy. Even these have their feebler imitators – a sort of sub-sub-cinema – but each remains supreme in its particular field.

Their films are seldom shown to the critics or given a West End run. Comparatively cheap to make, they can confidently rely on a profit. They employ a repertory of good actors and experienced technicians, who are expected to work with conveyor-belt regularity: on the set there is a minimum of that 'waiting about' traditionally associated with making films.

The Carry On comedies celebrate the schoolboy humour found in mildly vulgar postcards and 'comic-books', with jokes about underclothes and simple verbal confusions. The children who predominate in the audience for these U films would love to be smuggled past the X of the Hammer horrors. Here the rules are equally rigid: the scene is vaguely Hungarian, the period is vaguely *fin de siècle*, and the public is expected to know that vampires hate the sunlight, will not pass mirrors and can only be dispatched by a stake through the heart.

At Bray Studios, the Hammer horror factory, where the latest specimen, *The Gorgon*, was being made, the atmosphere was strikingly cosy: here film-making is a domestic affair, with family jokes and even a suggestion of nursery games. The producer, Anthony Nelson Keys (son of 'Bunch' Keys, the comedian) has a clown's kind, rubbery face: this is his first solo production, although as general manager of Bray Studios he has been involved in all the others. '*The Gorgon* is a bit subtler than the usual horror film,' he pointed out, 'because there isn't any blood. There's stone instead! We have a lot of fun making these films but we don't do them with our tongue in our cheek: we take them seriously. It's got to be *convincing* when Professor Heitz is turned to stone.'

The Gorgon is directed by Terence Fisher, who was responsible for the enormously successful *Curse of Frankenstein* and *Dracula*, as well as many of their successors. A shapeless, comfortable presence, he bustled gently about the set. This depicted the entrance hall of Castle Borski, home of the dreaded Gorgon, Megaera. Murky mirrors, broken statues, dusty tapestry, shattered stained glass, tattered flags, antlers and a tilted chandelier . . . all bathed in a green light, for green is the classic shade of horror and Hammer Films take pride in the quality of their colour. Cobwebs, spun from rubber solution, had been sprayed over the furniture. The Gorgon herself, incarnated by the actress Prudence Hyman, sat knitting in a deckchair, her face covered in hideous scales. She wore a dressing-gown, beneath which her winkle-pickers looked incongruously smart. Her wig, a triumph for 'special effects', with its tangle of serpents whose heads rear up, eyes light up and tongues protrude, was still in charge of the make-up man, Roy Ashton.

Ashton's room is the heart of Hammer. He sits here like a benevolent Nannie, surrounded by macabre models, detailed sketches, and the surprisingly innocent tools of his grisly trade. Grimacing masks hang round the walls, most of them identifiable: one, however, a revolting shrunken head, has never been used in a film. 'I just made that for fun one day, to amuse the company,' he said.

He displayed his creations with a craftsman's confident pride. 'Here is the mummy coming out of a swamp. Here is the werewolf. A man with slit ears. Dr Jekyll, from the famous story of *Dr Jekyll and Mr Hyde*. This is something I did for a thing called *Paranoiac*. These are sketches for *The Gorgon* – you see here that half her arm has fallen off. This series illustrates the whole progress of ossification. In the first one the fellow is all right. In the next he has holes in his head – it's all pitted, you see. Then here he is in his coffin, completely stone. I modelled that design on a photograph of Somerset Maugham.'

35

Meanwhile, Michael Goodliffe was on the set for the scene in which Professor Heitz encounters the Gorgon: he was made up to resemble the first sketch in Roy Ashton's series. The filming was itself being filmed, by a combined unit from Swiss and French TV which was preparing a documentary on horror films: there is a great cult for Hammer films on the Continent, particularly in Germany, and they are also very popular in Japan. When Goodliffe, rehearsing his close-up, let out a blood-curdling scream, there were exactly the same uneasy titters from the few spectators on the set as the episode will later provoke from cinema audiences. Then he turned slowly and staggered downstairs and out of the hall, his footsteps getting progressively heavier . . . These, however, will be dubbed. There is a girl who specialises in dubbing footsteps; she arrives with a bag full of shoes – everything from Army boots to ballet slippers – and puts on whichever fill the scene's requirements.

The Gorgon is the sixth Hammer film in which those key figures, Peter (Baron Frankenstein) Cushing and Christopher (Count Dracula) Lee have appeared together. Cushing's personality makes an effect of jocularity combined with tension. He entered the set with his body twisted into a grotesque distortion – a joke which went down well with the unit; when not before the camera, his handsome, intellectual features were occasionally animated by a nervous grimace. While acknowledging the lucrative aspect of horror movies ('There's gold in ghouls – particularly if they're gothic'), Cushing emphasises their quality: 'They have an authenticity all their own, like the best of grand guignol.' He hints at serious implications, and would like to apply Hitchcock's definition of *The Birds* as 'an attack on complacency' to Hammer films.

Christopher Lee takes this claim to significance even further. 'I try to emphasise the *loneliness* of evil,' he explained. 'Frankenstein's monster and the mummy didn't *ask* to be brought to life. Dracula couldn't help being like he was . . . I hate the word "horror". It doesn't mean any more than "western" or "musical". I prefer to call them fantasies – or, if you like, adult fairy tales.'

Lee is very tall, with a long face and sad dark eyes. He says

36

he never got big film parts before the monster in *The Curse of Frankenstein* because of his height – he made the leading man look small. 'Now that's typical of British movies. In Hollywood, with actors like Gary Cooper, John Wayne and Anthony Quinn, it wouldn't have mattered.' Lee is thinking of writing his auto-biography (possible title, *I'm All Right, Drac*), but is still pre-vented by the Official Secrets Act from describing his wartime experiences in Military Intelligence. Like everyone connected with the Hammer horror films, he adopts a slightly defensive attitude towards them: but he alone adds a strong element of aggression. 'I don't mind telling you that I resent the present trend in British movies. If there's a pile-up, it's their own fault. They should make films people want to see. Mind you, I haven't actually seen *Saturday Night and Sunday Morning* or *A Taste of Honey*, but from what I hear about these so-called realistic films, the men are either thugs or queers and the women look like whores. If I want to know about the boy and girl next door I can knock on the door. If I want to be sick I can go to a hospital.'

With Lee's apologia in mind, I read the first draft of John Gilling's screenplay for *The Gorgon*. Here is a scene laid in the laboratory of Professor Namaroff, the part played by Peter Cushing:

Namaroff has entered and has just switched on the light. In his hands he carries a box about a foot and a half square. He places the box on a bench in camera foreground. Now he opens the drawer of the bench and takes from it a chisel, a small hammer, and a surgeon's knife. He opens the lid of the box. We don't see what is inside at this moment but from Namaroff's expression we don't exactly get the impression that it is *pâté de foie gras*. Namaroff puts on a pair of rubber gloves. Now he begins very carefully to lift out the contents of the box. It is a *woman's severed head* . . . Namaroff places the head carefully on the bench, face upwards. He picks up his knife and makes a deep, clean incision starting from the crown of the head and carrying it almost as far as the bridge of the nose. Next he picks up the chisel and small hammer and pressing hard on the skull with the chisel he starts tapping steadily with the hammer . . . The head suddenly splits open and the grey mass of brains spills over on the bench . . . He smiles thinly.

NAMAROFF: It isn't a pretty sight. It never ceases to amaze me why the most noble work of God, the human brain, is the most revolting to the human eye.

The brains behind Hammer Films belong to the managing director, Colonel James Carreras. He is a showman by heredity: his father, Enrique Carreras, built the Blue Hall circuit of theatres and sponsored the first Royal Film Show – a performance of the silent *Quo Vadis* at the Albert Hall. Colonel Carreras (known in the war, when he commanded an anti-aircraft regiment, as 'Doodlebug Jim') is fifty-three, has a flat in Chester Street and a house in Brighton, plays golf to a six handicap, and is the only man to have been elected to the Chief Barkership of the Variety Club two years in succession. He rules his empire from Hammer House, Wardour Street.

He explained how he entered the horror field. 'In the fifties I started to exploit TV as I wanted a surefire certainty. So we made *The Man In Black, Dick Barton, P.C. 49* – all second features, and all subjects already made by the BBC. Then the BBC came along with *The Quatermass Experiment*. Everyone was after it, but as we'd been dealing with the BBC we got it and it was the biggest we'd ever had, our first film to be taken in America and get normal theatre bookings there. Now this was science fiction with a strong horror element. Then we got to talking about the old horror films, *Frankenstein* and *Dracula*, how they'd never been made in colour, and nobody had tried to revive them for twenty years. So in 1955 we made *The Curse of Frankenstein*. We only had the small sound-stage at Bray in those days, and the original budget was £80,000. Today it's gone up to £150,000, but this is still cheap, and we make good-looking pictures.

'*The Curse of Frankenstein* really went to town. It made fortunes overnight. It did well in America too, and you know what a difficult market that is for a British film. So we followed it up with *Dracula*. Since then we've remade practically all the classics – it's the classic does the business.'

In the language of horror films, 'classic' means any derivative from Mary Shelley or Bram Stoker (*The Revenge of Frankenstein, The Evil of Frankenstein, The Brides of Dracula*), several more or less original variations on similar themes (*The Curse of the Werewolf, The Kiss of the Vampire, The Blood of the Vampire, The Curse of the Mummy's Tomb*), and such adaptations from recognisable sources as *The Hound of the Baskervilles, Dr Jekyll and Mr Hyde, The Phantom of the Opera* and a projected version of *She*.

Colonel Carreras considers himself very lucky to have found a bread-and-butter formula. 'We have our own studios and control our own finance and we have distribution agreements with Columbia and Universal. At one time we made three horror films a year; now we average about two. After the first idea for a film is born, it's on the floor within six months. Shooting takes six to eight weeks, and about three months after that it's out. The so-called crisis doesn't affect us at all in getting the pictures made, though it may mean we have to wait longer for a release. I expect *The Gorgon* will be out some time in the autumn. We start getting our money back after the London release, and it comes back very quickly when you have a success. If we can get them into the London Pavilion, fine – otherwise we don't bother with the West End. We believe in following our product right the way through. Our manager incentive schemes offer prizes to managers who present our films with imagination, so the managers look forward to Hammer programmes. There's always some sort of angle you can exploit. When we gave a party to celebrate Tony Hinds's fiftieth production, we did up the Lancaster Room at the Savoy like Dracula's parlour, with skeletons and I don't know what else, and it made a very nice story.'

Hammer has three main sidelines: war pictures, pirate adventures and shock thrillers. 'Two of our war pictures were very successful, *The Camp on Blood Island* and *Yesterday's Enemy*,' said the Colonel. 'The Pirates are something else. It struck me there was a lot of business to pick up around the kids' holiday period – nobody had touched it except of course Disney, who had the field to himself. So we made *Pirates of Blood River* for the kids. In '62 we sent it out with *Mysterious Island* and they took more money than any other double feature that year. As for the thrillers: when *Psycho* was such a success – we like to think we're never far behind in following up good ideas – we made a quick series: *Scream of Fear, Maniac, Paranoiac, Nightmare*, and a whole batch of wonderful titles yet to come, let me see, *Hysteria*, *Brainstorm* and *The Reptiles*, that owes something to Hitchcock's *The Birds*. You have to couple two X films in a double feature, naturally, and we find one classic and one thriller make a good combination. *Kiss of the Vampire* and *Paranoiac* did well together, and next summer *Evil of Frankenstein* goes out with *Nightmare*. We even started to make comedies – *Up the Creek*, one of the first films to star Peter Sellers. It was very successful, but we're a bit out of our depth in comedy and *Further Up the Creek* (silly title) was a disaster.'

No doubt Colonel Carreras feels he can safely leave humour in the hands of another independent producer, Peter Rogers, who has made a similar killing with the 'Carry On' comedies. Rogers is married to Betty Box, who produces the rather more sophisticated and much more expensive 'Doctor' series, starring Dirk Bogarde: husband and wife have adjacent offices at Pinewood Studios. To add to the family connection, the director of the Carry Ons, Gerald Thomas, is the brother of Ralph Thomas, who directs the Doctors.

Carry On Spying is the ninth Carry On comedy in under seven years. The first, *Carry On Sergeant*, made in 1957, was swiftly followed by *Carry On Nurse*: this was the breakthrough picture, which was successful in America as well as at home. 'Nat Cohen and Stuart Levy of Anglo-Amalgamated took *Nurse* to the States and really flogged it,' I was told. Then came *Carry On Teacher*, *Carry On Constable*, *Carry On Regardless*, *Carry On Cruising*, *Carry On Cabby* and *Carry On Jack*, a satire on *Mutiny On the Bounty* with Kenneth Williams as a seasick captain, and a flogging scene in which the cat gets hopelessly entangled in the victim's long woollen vest. *Jack* starts its London release today, shooting on *Spying* is nearly finished, and later this year work begins on the tenth Carry On, 'about two stupid Ancient Britons who become slaves in Rome'. Opinion is divided as to whether it should be called *Carry On Caveman* or *Carry On Slave*: *Carry On Cleo* has been suggested, although it is feared this may be too much of an 'in-joke'.

Spying is a take-off of *Doctor No* and *From Russia With Love*: it features Charles Hawtrey as James Bind, Agent ooo (that's what they said when they saw him at BOSH – British Operational Security Headquarters). With Desmond Simkins (Kenneth Williams), Daphne Honeybutt (Barbara Windsor) and Harold Crump (Bernard Cribbins), he is sent after a secret formula stolen by STENCH (Society for the Total Extinction of Non-Conforming Humans), which is itself in competition with another sinister organisation called SMUT (Society for the Monopoly of Universal Technology). The action moves by trans-Continental express from the Café Mozart, Vienna, to the Casbah in Algiers, and contains such typical exchanges as these:

> BIND: Somebody just tried to shoot me.
> SIMKINS: Where?
> BIND: In the Schnitzelstrasse.
> SIMKINS: That sounds very painful!

and:

> POLICEMAN: What's going on here?
> CRUMP: (for some reason dressed as a woman) It's what's coming off that's worrying me!

The atmosphere on the Carry On set at Pinewood was even more homey than at Bray. Gerald Thomas, a mild figure in a raspberry-coloured sweater, has directed every one in the series; Kenneth Williams has been in all except *Cabby* and Charles Hawtrey in all except *Cruising. Spying*, however, is Barbara Windsor's first Carry On: Peter Rogers believes in introducing some new blood into the repertory with every film.

A general feeling of frustration at the embargo on really rude jokes imposed by the necessary U Certificate was eased by Kenneth Williams, whose first words on entering the set were: 'Have you heard the one about Christine Keeler getting her toe stuck in the bath-hole . . . ?' and who maintained a steady flow of anecdotes and imitations until work stopped at 5.50 p.m. 'The best jokes are off-screen,' said Gerald Thomas. 'Kenny's always like this, oh dear!' Barbara Windsor laughed so much that she had to be made up all over again. 'Isn't he *awful!*' she said, composing herself and sticking out her bosom ready for the take.

She was sitting at a table in the Café Mozart which bore a notice: 'Reserved for British Agents.' Everyone in the restaurant was a spy or counterspy; the scene showed the arrival of Bind, dressed as a Tour de France cyclist in spectacles, cap, multi-coloured singlet and leather shorts ('We're telling people they're Honor Blackman's knickers'). Charles Hawtrey as Bind had to dive into the *hors d'œuvres* trolley, which then crossed the room apparently under its own steam. Hawtrey had brought his mother on to the set, an old lady dressed in black, who sat by herself on the periphery, eating a tangerine, while he went through the scene.

Now and again an attempt has been made to vary the title of a Carry On film: *Cabby* was intended to be *Call Me A Cab*; *Spying* started life as *Come Spy With Me*. But the three magic syllables, applied to the standard formula, automatically please the box-office: so why change them? Peter Rogers cannot remember how he arrived at the phrase – 'It just happened.' When he experimented by putting the Carry On team in *Twice Round the Daffodils*, it failed. 'This was the only instance where the critics affected the box-office take,' he said. 'They thought it was bad taste making a comedy about TB – but TB is curable now. I wouldn't make one about cancer. And some people said about *Nurse*: "Fancy making fun of hospitals," but the truth is that people do get an awful lot of fun in hospitals.'

Peter Rogers has produced more than forty films. 'I started in country journalism, wrote plays before the war, and went into films as a dialogue writer: people liked my dialogue but not my plays! In '42 I joined Rank's religious outfit, writing religious films. Then I went into Fleet Street – if there hadn't been a war on and a shortage of men they'd never have taken me on as a journalist, I'm much too lazy and I hate moving about. I worked on *Picture Post* till I was kicked out by Ted Carson, then I joined *World's Press News*. Then back to Rank, writing things like *The Huggetts*. I was working at the old Islington studios with my wife – Betty was producing and I was scripting – when there was another so-called film crisis: they happen every so often, you know. So we threw in our lot together and made a dramatic thriller called *The Clouded Yellow* – my first production, and very successful.

'For two years I took the Carry On idea round to different people and nobody wanted it. Then I came across Nat Cohen and Stuart Levy, and they had the courage to believe in it too; they got *Sergeant* a distribution on the ABC circuit, so I've stayed with Anglo-Amalgamated ever since. The Carry Ons do well in Australia and New Zealand, but in France they prefer the more whimsy humour of the Ealing comedies. Of course our greatest following is among the very young – we get lots of letters from kids in America. They love them there because they're so British. Why try to make big pictures like the Americans? Mine don't pretend to be American. How do you account for the success of the E-type Jaguar? Because it's small, and British.'

Like the Hammer horrors, the Carry Ons stemmed indirectly from TV. 'I used some TV characters in *Sergeant*, from *The Army Game* and that kind of thing, and in this respect TV virtually advertised my pictures for nothing,' said Rogers. 'In the early days we made three a year – you have to hit the public on the head so fast, bang bang bang, that they get used to the idea – but this year we're only making two. I hear of other producers complaining of a £250,000 budget for one picture, but I could make two for that. Gerry Thomas is very budget-conscious, and that helps. They've all been black and white, except for *Cruising* and *Jack*.'

The earning potential of all the Carry Ons is much the same; naturally it is the early ones like *Sergeant* and *Nurse*, which have been reissued, that have made most money to date. Shooting takes six weeks, and a Carry On is ready to go out in about nine months – 'But we often rush a thing through in four. We sometimes get our money back on the London release alone; after that, it's all profit. I don't go in for gloss, like Betty does with the Doctors, but I do go in for competence: I employ some of the best (and most expensive!) technicians in the business. I seldom bother with West End runs now. The West End audience is extremely difficult – you get people shopping for films there more than they did.

'I know at once if a thing will make a Carry On. I give the writers the story in outline, and then it's part of my job as producer to rewrite a scene when necessary. I find you can't get rid of the writing bug once you've had it! I love the team-work. None of the actors is highspotted at the expense of the others, so you don't get the upstaging you find elsewhere. Their prices have spiralled since we started, but if they're worth it they're worth it. But it must stay at a certain level – if an artist goes beyond that I let him go, or you have the tail wagging the dog. But I never interfere with an artist's work. You wouldn't say to Kenneth Williams or Barbara Windsor: "Do this another way" – they have their own. When you're buying someone's personality it's pointless to try and change it.'

Peter Rogers speaks in soft, measured tones and gives an impression of slightly studied dignity. He has a passion for dogs, especially setters and Alsatians, and his office at Pine-wood is filled with representations of these breeds: photographs, paintings, drawings, statuettes in china, silver and bronze. Drummer's Yard, the vast house at Beaconsfield which he bought from Dirk Bogarde, is a stately cross between a Spanish monastery, a medieval fortress and the furniture department at Harrods. Here the grounds are filled with live animals, rescued from slaughter by Peter Rogers – a rare breed of Highland cattle, a pit pony, a donkey. The donkey had belonged to a milkman who intended to destroy it because of its bad temper. Rogers heard that a little girl had saved up her sweet money to buy the donkey, but it proved to be too bad-tempered for the little girl, whom it ungratefully tried to bite: so he bought it from her. Until recently his favourite pets were two Alsatians, Rex and Timba. When Timba fell ill he carpeted the whole patio to make a sickroom. After Timba had to be put to sleep he bought another Alsatian, Simba, and he leaves the set of *Spying* early every day in order to get to know the new puppy.

Kenneth Williams had suggested that the Carry Ons were a film equivalent to the Whitehall farces (*One for the Pot*, etc.) but Rogers did not agree. 'The Carry Ons are quite unlike any other British comedy I can remember. One critic referred to them as "fat-headed farces" – fat-headed, perhaps, but I object to farce. There is never much logic in a farce, and we have to have logic in a Carry On to make it appear possible. They are neither farce nor satire; we make a point of having nothing cruel in the humour. We're giving them a little bit of a facelift at present by concentrating more on the story line. This creates its own problems, of course – you can't cut to make the film go faster because you might miss a story point.

'I have a second line of production, making more dramatic subjects. But with business as it is, all the exhibitors want is comedy, because it is safe. I believe in staying in your own pasture. You play safe in the comedy rut. If I want to do other pictures I realise I must put them aside. My own aim is to please, to try to make people laugh. I believe you should put the customers first, the audience before the critics, and I find the customers have got a little bit tired of seeing people wrapped up in sheets in bed. We try only to make *happy* pictures. I don't like anything sick.'

The climactic scene of *Carry On Jack* concerns an amputation, that old standby for sick humour. Yet Rogers is right: the situation is treated in a way peculiar to Carry On comedy.

'His foot's gone a funny colour. I don't like the look of it.'
'Neither do I. I never did care for green.'

And:

'I shall need a saw, a knife, a needle and thread.'
'Who's Fred?'

The very feebleness of the punning takes the sickness out of the joke. Some people may think it also takes out the joke – yet at the trade show this scene got louder laughter than any other.

'I wouldn't be so mad as to say I'd rather do something else,' Peter Rogers summed up; and he can be taken as speaking for the sub-cinema as a whole. He was anxious to distinguish his own taste from that of his product. 'I couldn't live without *Punch* coming every week into my house and I'm very proud of my bound set. But in the film business you must be faithful to two people – the bank, and the customer: if you try pleasing yourself, you've had it. I try to be faithful to my customers. If I said we must do this, that or the other thing, they'd run away. It's like meeting someone in the bar for a drink – and telling him what he's got to have! After all, film-making is a form of shopkeeping: and I'm very proud to hear the bell.'

1964

Hylda At Home

THE FRONT DOOR WAS OPENED BY HYLDA BAKER HERSELF. SHE
was dabbing at her bosom with some expensive-looking
scent. 'I had to go and drop this boiling fat on the front of my
dress just before you came and I can't get it out. Of course, in
my young days they called this stuff toilet-water, which is what
it is, but now they say it's perfume and it costs five times as
much. Come in, dear. Hang up your coat in this wardrobe but
mind you don't get your fingers squeezed in the door. You
must excuse me if everything's a little confused, but you see
I'm all on my lonesome, by myself, alone. Oh yes, I'm advertising like mad for a housekeeper and a maid, but they don't want
to know, do they? It's when you've been poorly, as I have
lately, that you find out who your real friends are. You see, I've
had a bit of a spasm. I was up till four or five in the morning
judging this talent contest, and I didn't feel so well when I got
back home because of the ordeal or whatever, and you know
when you say "I think I'll have a whisky and soda" – or it might
be a gin and tonic, or a vodka and something – and you see I
only drink (terrible, isn't it?) champagne, that's doctor's orders
– well, I think something like that must have happened. And
does anybody come? No. I don't think they want to know,
they've enough troubles of their own. You're quite right to say
you're lucky if you've one *real* friend. Which I thought I had . . .
Well, this stain doesn't seem to be coming out. I'll cover it up
with my Bolton Wanderers rosette.'

The telephone rang. 'Hullo? No I am not, you have a wrong
number! Foiled again! "Are you Foyle's?" Happens all the time,
I think I'll leave it off the hook . . . Do you divulge?' she asked
in the outlandish tones of Nellie Pickersgill (manageress of the
Brown Cow pub in her television series *Not on Your Nellie*), as
she almost disappeared from view behind a small, neat bar.
A mirror on the wall above her had her two most famous

47

catchphrases ('She knows, you know' and 'Be soon') written on the glass, and a set of brown cocktail-sticks stuck on the top. These showed, in silhouette, a naked African woman at different ages, her breasts progressively sagging. 'That's Zulu Lulu – she's a bit naughty, I'm afraid. She comes from the Continent – as you can well imagine! Do you like this little cocktail glass? Artistic, isn't it? It was one of a pair. Somebody gave me them as a present – they're hand-made, you know, from what's-it-called, I can't remember the name of the country, never mind – and I'm sorry to say that the other one was *purloined*. Oh yes! I must have a word with the head porter about that. I don't mean he took it, certainly not, but he brought them up, you see, he let them in. There's a communal aerial in this block of flats and some of them wanted to listen to the what-do-you-call-it on my set. You know, the thingum-myjig, what *is* it called, when all the Government was on? *Her*, Mrs what's-her-name. That's right, dear, the *election*. Well, they came up to watch it while I wasn't here and I believe one of them must have purloined my little what's-it. I wouldn't mind so much if it wasn't one of a pair. Never mind. "An evening spent with Hannah in a big armchair, is like walking through Alaska in your underwear . . ." Oh! I've accused that man, and here it is! I've just found it on the floor. Isn't it lovely hand-carving? I think it must belong to the Ming dysentery . . . '

Hylda Baker came out from behind the bar, struck an attitude and began to declaim: ' "Under the starlight glitter, Stands a little fragile girl, Heedless of the night winds bitter, As they round about her whirl . . ." Oh yes, I used to do all that rubbish. I really always wanted to be a dramatic actress. Some-body said I had magnetism – I said "I don't know what you mean, but I like the way you said it!" Mind you, I like cheerful music too.' She sat at the piano and played 'A Good Man is Hard to Find' followed by her own version of 'I'm a Little on the Lonely Side'. ' "To the altar, I had to falter, and promised I would be his bride. He cut a dash, with all my cash . . . " As my sister used to say, when I had that terrible illness that lasted eight months, you're so cheerful nobody would know you had anything wrong with you. I said, why should I depress other people? I know what would happen if I did. Sorry I can't say hullo – and not half! – because I'll be on my way, Lily.

'See that picture on the piano? That's me with Lew Grade and Bernie Delfont, who are very good friends of mine. And here I am in my drawing room when I was topping the bill for two months at the Prince of Wales. And I've appeared before Her Majesty, you know. *Oh*, yes! Much better than the Royal Command Performance – much! Because you see I had all four of them. I had Queen Elizabeth and Prince Philip and Prince Charles and Princess what's-her-name? Anne. It was some charity, something to do with the army, I think. I was introduced to them later, like you are, you know. I did my curtsey and I said: "Excuse me, Queen, but did you happen to see my friend? She was in the taxi just after yours." That's from my act with Cynthia, you know, it goes on: "She's tall and blonde with aquamarine features and she wears her hair in a nutcracker suite. She looks a bit like Gina Lollobrigadier." I heard afterwards they fell about. "Most enjoyable," the Queen said. So now in my act I always say: "As the Queen told me – *most* enjoyable!"

'And here on the piano is the book they give you when you've been on *This Is Your Life*. Oh, I went all jelly when I realised I was on! There we all are doing the clog dance. There's a sister. More sisters. Sisters. Sisters. I come from a family of seven, you know. Here I am with Cynthia, she was meant to be deaf, you know, and never spoke. I've kept that up ever since – I've got Gilbert now in *Not on Your Nellie*, he never speaks either, does he? That's Barney Colehan who put my Cynthia act in *The Good Old Days* on telly, oh, twenty years ago it must be, and made me a star overnight. A bit late to be a star overnight – I'd been on the stage for thirty years already! Mind you, I started when I was ten. (And I could do six steps and a shuffle when I was three.) Yes, Cynthia was played by a boy then. I used different people. It was meant to be a secret who they were till some idiot blabbed his big mouth off, to make something of himself, I suppose, which was rickidoodalous. I mean, it was just Cynthia, it didn't matter who wore the clothes, she never says anything, does she? All she has to do is just stand there, looking gormless.

'That's my aunt who's always been very good to me. She's died since then. And my cousin. Eamonn Andrews flew her all the way over from America for the show. She tried to tell that story about me and the fish-knives. You see, I was in a very expensive restaurant in America and I was so shocked that they didn't have fish-knives, I said it was like a fish and chip shop. My family had a fish and chip shop in Farnworth, you know. Anyway, she tried to tell the story but she got in such a muddle at the rehearsal that they cut it down to a few seconds and we said was it really worth it flying her all that way? And that's Dot Squires. She came along. I used to know her when she was Billy Reid's vocalist. Later they became co-stars and they topped the bill at the Palladium, but they had some sort of disagreement. Then she was on her own till she met Roger Moore. She was very upset when that trouble happened there. I used to go down and try to make her laugh, because it hit her very hard. We're very close friends – in trouble, not just when things go well. I've known a lot of trouble myself, you know. That's when you need friends, and you find you've got nobody.

'And this is the Hammer Film man. I was to do *The Godmother*, you know. Oh, yes. I think I know what went wrong. Because we couldn't get a certain person. That big Scotch fellow – I can't remember his name. They'd announced it and everything – "Hylda Baker is going to be The Godmother" – and they'd made up their minds where they were going to put him. Then he became a star. You know who I mean – with the chair – "Shut that door". But I'm not supposed to even know why it didn't come off. Here's a fan letter I got from a little girl of nine. "This is just a letter to tell you I think you are very good and very funny and my mummy and daddy think so too. I look forward to The Brown Cow every week. My mummy says you have a go at anything, you are smashing!" There! What can't speak can't lie! That proves I appeal to all ages. The first time I used "rickidoodalous" there were these two little boys waiting outside the flat and they said: "Miss (what do they call me?) Nellie, do say rickidoodalous for us." So I stood there like a mug and said, "Don't be rickidoodalous!" Oh well, whether you like it or not, there's somebody that does. Or so it seems.

'This sheet music on the piano is the theme song I wrote for

Not on Your Nellie, but it's only handwritten so I don't think I can play it for you. I don't know where I put my spectacles, to tell you the truth. I wanted them to bring it out as a single, with a nice honky-tonk pub piano background. Well, it's taken them long enough, they've had it twelve months. They told me it would cost a thousand pounds to make and I said don't be so daft. Yes, written *and* composed by Hylda Baker – she was always very quick at composition when she was at school, was our Hylda. "No – not on your Nellie!" Oh, I've written a lot of songs and I've never done anything about them. 'My Home Town', I wrote that. I write songs for my act, and I write my own patter, and I wrote my own revues – no, dear, not *reviews*, or I'd have made myself a star thirty years earlier! And, of course, my representation of a mute in each one as a continuation of Cynthia – that's my own thing. And that, too, was mine: "And how are you today? Oh, you're one of those, are you?" I wanted Gilbert and George to be ton-up boys, I thought that would be funnier, but Mr What's-it thought he'd put them in silver and gold.

'I've got to stay in London till Tuesday because I've got an appointment on Tuesday. Then I'm free. I think I'll take a holiday. I need one. I thought I was free today, but they can't make up their minds about how much money I want for the next series. What they offered wasn't quite what I expected. So I kept quiet about it and told them what I did expect. They bought me a very nice lunch. But they needn't have bothered, really, because I'll get what I asked for in the end. "Roll me over, lay me down and do it again!" '

The front-door bell rang and Hylda Baker spoke down a tube connected with the street door. 'It's the lodger, he says! He's coming round about the cars . . . Come in, Dennis. Did you walk up the stairs or take the bus? Would you like a drink?'

'Twist my arm,' said Dennis.

'Well, I can't reach across the bar that far . . . Oh, are you going, then? Bye-bye, dear. Be soon.'

The hour I spent with Hylda Baker in her spotless home near the Tottenham Court Road had somehow reminded me of the last few minutes in a pub before closing time, when the atmosphere of jollity intensifies to an almost dangerous degree

51

and everything seems to be hovering on the brink of getting out of control: drinks are spilled, saucy or sentimental tunes are sung over a loud piano that isn't quite in tune, and intimacies are struck up which are immediately forgotten. A star who will countenance no co-star – and who is even slightly suspicious of her supporting cast – she turns one into an admiring audience who is also, like Cynthia, a happily speechless stooge. What makes her comic performance so unique? Partly her voice, strangulated between robust North Country vulgarity and a peculiar camp refinement; partly her odd, fractured timing (which is much funnier than the verbal confusions that are her stock in trade); partly the vehement exaggeration of her gestures, which agitate every inch of her tiny body; and partly, beneath the lapses of memory and the near-hysterical vagueness, the suggestion of a shrewd, cynical appreciation of the failings of the human race. She may be the broadest of low comediennes, but one can be reminded of her on unexpected occasions. For example, in Benjamin Britten's opera based on Thomas Mann's *Death in Venice*, Peter Pears as the ageing Aschenbach, lusting after the beautiful Polish youth, reiterates a phrase from Myfanwy Piper's libretto: 'He's notices when he's noticed.' Did anyone connected with this impeccably highbrow production realise that he was echoing the immortal words of Hylda Baker? 'She knows, you know.'

1975

LOVE DUET

'OH, MY CRINS!' SAID ANNE ZIEGLER. 'DO YOU REALLY remember my crins? They *were* rather gorgeous, weren't they? My favourite was the white with a huge pink rose at one side of the bodice – the stalk and the leaves were embroidered on the material. But I'm afraid they're all in store now. We just don't have room for them here.'

'Of course, my biggest tragedy,' said Webster Booth, 'is that I ever parted with my beautiful tails. I gave them away in South Africa – thought I'd never need them again. I should have realised they were irreplaceable. Prices are terrible here, aren't they? It would cost me hundreds of pounds to get a decent suit of tails now. These were made for me, you know, specially fitted, oh, years and years ago. I sometimes feel I should write to the chap and say "If you don't want them, I'll pay you anything to have them back." '

Anne's crinoline dresses with long lace sleeves, and Webster's tail suits with a gardenia buttonhole, were almost as essential to their success as their soprano and tenor voices, which combined so effectively in love duets from operettas and the popular classical repertoire. The numbers most frequently requested in their heyday (between the late 1930s and the early 1950s) were 'One Fine Day' from Anne, 'The Lord's Prayer' from Webster and 'We'll Gather Lilacs' from them both.

He came from Birmingham, served an apprenticeship with the D'Oyly Carte opera company and started a career as a serious concert performer. She was born Irene Eastwood in Liverpool, began as a pianist and then sang in pantomime and musical comedy. They met in a studio while making a film of Gounod's *Faust*. After Webster Booth had been divorced by his first wife, he married Anne Ziegler on 5 November, 1938. This set the seal on a romantic partnership which was to delight an enormous audience until *The Vagabond King* and *Waltz Time* were superseded in the affections of the middlebrow public by *My Fair Lady* and *The Sound of Music*.

Radio was their main medium, although they also made appearances on the stage and in front of the early television cameras. In 1956 they left Britain for South Africa ('There was no Palladium for us in those days, it was all rock 'n' roll') where they ran a School of Singing and Stagecraft in Johannesburg. Earlier this year, they came back home. I found them in a bungalow at Penrhyn Beach, a windy stretch of ribbon development along the North Welsh coast between Llandudno and Colwyn Bay.

'This weather – what a shocker!' said Webster Booth as we passed through a narrow hall into a small, bright living room. A tall, imposing figure, with a rather absent manner, he speaks slowly and seldom, suggesting a genial, easy-going nature with a vague hint of sardonic amusement beneath his reserve. His wife, by contrast, is vivid and volatile, chattering impulsively and laughing often; her smile is still brilliant, illuminating her blonde good looks which (like those of Anna Neagle and Evelyn Laye) are in the essentially English style admired in the 1930s.

'Not much that you see here belongs to us,' she said. 'Very little is allowed out of South Africa, you know, and we had to leave a lot of stuff behind.'

'Couldn't afford to ship the heavy furniture all the way back,' muttered Webster Booth.

But the room bore traces of their occupancy. On the piano: their wedding photograph and the scores of *Faust*, *Bohème*, Mendelssohn's *Elijah* and Handel's *Messiah*. On the coffee table, which was decorated by black minims and semi-quavers on a white background: a copy of their joint autobiography, *Duet* (Stanley Paul, 1951) and a pile of LPs – *Sweethearts of Song, Love Duets from Theatreland* and a collection of Webster Booth's solos reissued by EMI last year. On the walls: a diploma commemorating their appearance at a Royal Command Performance, watercolours of Canadian and South African landscapes, two flower paintings on silk. 'Those are by my mother,' said Anne Ziegler. 'That's one thing I've always longed to do – paint. How lovely to put something down and know it's there for good! But I just don't have the gift. And I love good food, but for the life of me

I just can't cook. Thank God I've got a husband who can!'

'And thank God I've got a wife who can garden.'

'We had such a heavenly garden in S.A. – that is, until we had to pack it in, sell the house and move to a block of flats in Jo'burg. We just couldn't get the labour to keep it up. But I do miss that garden. This place isn't ours, you see. It belongs to my life-long girlfriend. She came to our rescue and saved our lives! She has a place in Southport, but we thought that was *too* far away, so she let us move in here. Babs Wilson-Hill – I first met her in panto (well, there's no point in lying about my age, is there?) back in 1935, the year after I left Liverpool. I was the principal boy and she danced – Babs was *the* most beautiful dancer! That was my first big date – apart from meeting this old boy in a film studio, of course! George Formby and George Lacey were in the cast – I remember the two Georges were so jealous of each other, they fought like cat and dog! I loved panto – but I do think you *must* have a woman to play the boy. It doesn't seem right, somehow, now they've started having the boys done by men.'

'I'm sorry to say that the custom has even spread to South Africa now,' said Webster Booth.

'Mind you, I would like to make it clear that we did *not* leave because of the political situation over there,' said Anne Ziegler. 'No it was more – well, homesickness, really.'

'We felt we wanted to get back to our roots,' said Webster Booth. 'We never stop being glad we're back. We wouldn't say a word against South Africa – we made many friends out there – but somehow we didn't put our roots down, I don't know why.'

'Without being a snob,' said Anne Ziegler, 'I think I'd say that the thing we missed most in Jo'burg was the cultural side of life. That Equity business, or whatever it is, stops so much that is good from coming over. And their TV is an absolute tragedy – though they've just had *Royal Heritage*, thank God! But we kept busy. We had our singing studio for eleven years. We produced amateur shows. We sang with two choral societies. We did lots of radio stuff. And we acted together in *The Amorous Prawn* and *Goodnight Mrs Puffin*.'

'The only thing I miss now is their fruit,' said Webster Booth.

'You could get sixty grapefruit for 40 pence when we left in January. But their meat was very bad – they've nothing to eat, poor things!'

'But the price of food in this country!' said Anne Ziegler. 'By the way, what is *coley*? One never heard of it in the old days, but now it seems the only thing one can afford.'

'Used to give it to cats.'

'Of course, I couldn't possibly have come back until after my last baby died. She was a little cairn bitch called Silver – he gave it to me for our silver wedding. And I used to have a Maltese terrier which followed me around like a shadow – couldn't even spend a penny without it! People think I'm mad, I know, but I don't. When our two cats had to be put to sleep, Webster took them to the vet – and we never discussed it for six months! I never had children, you see. Webster has a son and two grandchildren by his first marriage, but I always said a career *and* children was out of the question, I just wouldn't do it.'

'We've given a few concerts since we've been home,' said Webster Booth. 'One at Stevenage – the theatre looked like a factory. The Dome at Brighton. St Helens – though you needed a compass to find it. A lot of that we owe to Jess Yates – you know, he used to do *Stars on Sunday*. He lives just down the road from here, actually.'

'We had a standing ovation at the Eisteddfod at Cardiff. There were 4500 people there – it was fantastic. Webster's given recitals at Lewisham and Edmonton.'

'Edmonton, England, that is. I did a D'Oyly Carte Canadian tour in 1926 when Calgary was just a cow town and Edmonton hadn't been built. And do you remember that fabulous *Merrie England* job in Canada? They flew us over to Calgary just for one performance, then up to the Rockies for the weekend.'

'I shall never forget the *Merrie England* we did at Luton Hoo in Coronation year,' said Anne Ziegler. 'There were 1000 in the cast and I think there was seating for 7000 people. The Luton Girls' Choir was with us. It was all out of doors.'

'And it rained every night, or nearly . . . I think I must have been pretty well everywhere except out East. I've always had a feeling that the Far East was *dirty*. People who go there say it's wonderful, but I don't know . . . '

'I'd love to go back to New Zealand for a visit,' said Anne Ziegler. 'Not that I want to go away again, anywhere. But it's so beautiful. I prefer it to Australia myself. I always think Australia's a *man's* country. As for Rhodesia – don't let's mention *that* tragedy!'

They changed out of day clothes to be photographed, and Webster Booth began again to bemoan the loss of his tails. 'They were made by Sterman and Mason – we'll never see their like again! It just never entered my head that this would happen and we'd have to go back on the stage. I thought they're really not worth keeping, we can't go on singing for *very* much longer. But I think we've found a tame tailor now in Colwyn Bay . . . this morning coat will have to do.'

'You have lost weight, haven't you?' said Anne Ziegler.

'Well, what do you expect? Look at the label – 1949! Just shows that some stuff always lasts. Here, feel it – good as new!'

'I wore this at the Eisteddfod at Cardiff,' said Anne Ziegler. 'It's a bit crushed but that won't show. All I can say is, thank God for drip-dry!'

'You mean the seagull one?'

'No, darling, the pink one.'

'You hadn't got that on at the Eisteddfod.'

'Darling, while you were doing the introduction I rushed off the stage, took off the seagull and had this pink job on underneath. You must have noticed.'

'Can't see a thing without my spectacles.'

'I'll tell you a gorgeous story about Malcom Sargent,' said Anne Ziegler. 'Webster's togs have just reminded me. Well, we'd both been to Ascot and we went straight on out to dinner in the West End. Sargent was sitting in the restaurant – he'd just been knighted, so Webster went over to his table to congratulate him. He looked up and he said: "And who have you been marrying today?" Oh, he was a monster! But what a showman, too. The most careful accompanist in the world – with you in his hands, you knew you just couldn't go wrong.'

'Don't talk about accompanists. They're another thing you can't get now. In our act, ideally, the accompanist should be part of the trio.'

'I suppose we were spoilt. We first had Charles Forwood – he played for us for fourteen years. And my boyfriend, Ivor Newton – we saw a lot of him in s.a. – he's a darling. Ivor and Gerald Moore were the great ones, weren't they?'

'Gerald wrote a book called *Am I Too Loud?*' said Webster Booth. 'I always wanted to say, "Yes, much!" '

'I sometimes accompanied the old boy myself at functions, when *he* was the big bug. But when you've had the best, it's very difficult, isn't it? We had a very good one the other day, though. Tessie O'Shea was on the bill with us. A little Viennese Jewess called Beata Popperwell played for us – she was fabulous. Two rehearsals, and we didn't know she was there. I can't play by ear, you know. I've played all my life, but I'm *useless* without the music! And I feel such a *prune*!'

'These might interest you,' said Webster Booth, producing two more LPs. 'This one called *Famous Tenors* – I knew them all personally.'

'You see, I *hate* tenors – isn't it dreadful?' said his wife. 'Apart from this old boy here, of course – he's the exception! But I always tell him I *much* prefer baritones, don't I, darling?'

'And this is a record of us with the sleeve notes in Afrikaans.'

'I always think things said in Afrikaans sound so *rude*!' said Anne Ziegler. 'I only learned a few words of it, but I never dared open my mouth!'

'We still take pupils, when we can find them,' said Webster Booth. 'We've had one, a young man of only twenty-four, who's really outstanding. He's been in a concert party show at Llandudno, so of course he'll be moving away soon. Going into opera, the real thing. An extraordinary bass-baritone voice, he's got. The Welsh are known to be the most musical people in the world, aren't they? There's a lot of very good music round here. And we're quite near the Welsh Opera. On my birthday we went to see Geraint Evans in *A Midsummer Night's Dream* – now there's a voice for you! But otherwise there's not much doing up here, really.'

'But the people round here are fabulous,' said Anne Ziegler. 'There is *something* about North Country folk. They'd do anything for you. And, of course, to be called "luv" again in the shops simply thrills me! Oh, I adore it, I think it's marvellous!'

'It's a good place to retire to. But the trouble is, we haven't retired.'

'We can't sing love duets, not at our ages,' said Anne Ziegler. 'A couple of old geezers like us doing "Lover Come Back to Me" or "You, Just You"! So we've worked up a kind of patter – a bit jokey and a bit nostalgic. We do "I Remember it Well", then "The Keys of Heaven" (which we burlesque) and end up with "Wunderbar". It seems to go down well.'

'But it's rather difficult – the expense of it,' said Webster Booth. 'The cost of travel and the hotel bills – and hiring tails is so dear. And then on top of that we have to pay VAT on our agent's commission. We don't really understand about VAT – they didn't have it in S.A., though now I believe they've imposed one at four per cent. And I'm told there are certain benefits we can claim as old age pensioners . . . we'll have to find out about that.'

'Just so long as people know we're back,' said Anne Ziegler. 'Your article will help to remind them, won't it? Bring it out on Bonfire Night and say, "Haven't they changed after forty years!" '

I was able to reply quite truthfully that I thought they had hardly changed at all.

1978

THE DISCREET CHARM OF
STÉPHANE AUDRAN

ALTHOUGH THE NAME OF STÉPHANE AUDRAN IS NOT YET widely known outside her native France, this fascinating actress enjoys a submerged reputation among a growing band of film fans in Britain and America. Writing about her in the *New York Times* early last year, Vincent Canby described his 'immediate awareness that here is someone unique . . . She possesses a quality I promise not to ascribe to anyone else within the next five years – namely, glamour. She is elegant, funny, wise, foolish, distant, possessed, at loose ends, sometimes all within a single scene.'

Canby claims that she is 'the kind of old-fashioned movie star everyone says they don't make like they used to', but points out that she is also a far better actress than many of the Hollywood movie queens of the 1930s. It is true that she appeals, as they did, both sexually to men and socially to women – but to me she is less a descendant of the Crawford–Stanwyck–Lombard tradition than of their Parisian contemporaries: cool, sceptical Arletty; exquisite, enigmatic Michèle Morgan; scintillating, vulnerable Danielle Darrieux. She probably has a wider range than any of these earlier stars, but like them she encompasses it within a definite and clearly identifiable personality.

Stéphane Audran seems the embodiment of the smart French bourgeoise, the kind of woman you would want to sit at the head of your table in the 16th *arrondissement* among the wrought iron and the Bernard Buffets, to accompany you on your skiing holiday in Mégève, to do the honours among your banker friends. At the same time she suggests the tactful mistress, eminently desirable because her sensual needs are so skilfully concealed beneath a civilised composure. Imbuing the vocation of hostess with erotic undertones, she is a classic French type, both practical and passionate. Her haunting face, so carefully controlled that it almost resembles a mask, can reveal doubt, desire or despair by the smallest shift of expression in her handsome eyes; her lovely smile may betoken ecstatic joy or mere good manners. Her walk is superb: graceful, athletic, and somehow formal, as if she were presenting herself on a tray. The reverse of arty, she has nothing in common with the neurotic whimsy and fashionable *je m'en foutisme* of the latest brand of French actresses, wayward moderns like Maria Schneider and Dominique Sanda. Her screen characterisations suggest a disciplined nature, conformist and perhaps even a shade philistine. As she is in fact an extremely talented, witty and sensitive artist, the effect is subtly exciting.

She was born at Versailles about forty years ago. Although she studied acting under such distinguished teachers as Charles Dullin, Tania Balachova and Michel Vitold, her early stage career was modest: Racine *confidantes* at provincial drama festivals, small parts on television. Her screen debut was in 1959, when she made brief appearances in four films. One of these was *Les Cousins*, the second film directed by Claude Chabrol, to whom she had been introduced by the actor Gérard Blain. (This was the time, if you can bear to be reminded of the fact once again, when Chabrol, Truffaut, Godard, Rohmer and other critics-turned-directors were launching the phenomenon known as the *Nouvelle Vague*: Chabrol is acknowledged as having pioneered the movement with *Le Beau Serge* in 1958.) Pleased with her work, Chabrol gave her an important role in his fourth film, *Les Bonnes Femmes*. Since its appearance in 1960 she has made nineteen more movies, all but six of them directed by Chabrol, whom she married in 1964. In that year, he also directed her as Lady Macbeth in a stage production which failed to please the French critics and public.

Stéphane Audran's beauty, her clean-cut style and distinctive charm, were apparent in all her films, but it was not until *Les Biches* in 1968 that she was given a chance to realise her full potential as an actress. In this disturbing, rather cruel work, she plays Frédérique, an attractive, embittered woman who picks up a young girl at Saint Tropez, seduces her and turns her into a kind of slave. When the girl has an affair with a man,

Frédérique seduces him too, and is eventually murdered by her victim. Stéphane Audran's remarkably subtle performance, which manages to be ambiguous without ever becoming blurred, was rightly awarded the Best Actress prize at the Berlin Film Festival. Her next movie, *La Femme Infidèle*, had the most banal of plots: a husband discovers that his wife is deceiving him, and kills her lover. Here again, subtlety came to the rescue: under Chabrol's direction, Stéphane Audran and that brilliant actor Michel Bouquet provided a definitive analysis of the complex tensions within a bourgeois marriage.

It was now clear to most film critics that Stéphane Audran had an unusual gift for giving complete credibility to the most hackneyed or bizarre situations. Her unique talent was further tested in *Le Boucher*, where she plays a provincial schoolmistress involved with a sex murderer; in *La Rupture*, where an innocent wife and mother undergoes a series of Gothic ordeals; and in *Juste Avant la Nuit*, where a quintessentially bourgeoise matron serenely forgives her husband's infidelity and then receives the news that he is a murderer without turning a hair of her elaborate orange *coiffure*. The tests were triumphantly passed; indeed, it might be said of these Chabrol films that the best thing about them is the acting of his wife. Their most recent collaboration, *Les Noces Rouges*, is yet another drama of bourgeois respectability imperilled by adultery and murder.

After making *La Femme Infidèle*, Stéphane Audran began being professionally unfaithful to her husband with other directors, but all the results were undistinguished until last year. Then Luis Buñuel gave her a leading role in his masterpiece, *The Discreet Charm of the Bourgeoisie*. If Chabrol, obsessed by the bourgeoisie, had been trying to undermine its values while apparently celebrating them in lovingly recorded detail, the seasoned Spanish surrealist now mounted a frontal attack, using every weapon from fantasy to farce. The long apprenticeship in her husband's films stood Stéphane Audran in good stead: those endless scenes at the dining table, the gracious offering of a *framboise* to a boring guest, the conventionally elegant clothes, the keeping up of appearances, the brisk delivery of social banalities, the complicit cover-up of lust and violence by an almost fanatical concentration on style in domestic decor and the right brand of consumer goods – her training had been thorough and she had won her diploma. French to her fingertips, she was alive to every nuance of 'taste'. Like a time-fuse that had been politely sizzling through the Chabrol years, her performance under Buñuel exploded with the force of an anarchist's bomb.

When I wrote to her, Stéphane Audran was on holiday in the Gironde with her ten-year-old son, Thomas. In her reply she gave me a rendezvous for the end of July at her house in Neuilly. I was prepared for disappointment: so often one sets out to meet an image, and discovers just an actress. It was Sunday; the city was stale, preparing for its *fermeture annuelle*; it was four o'clock when I reached the affluent, shady suburb, pushed open the iron gate, crossed the front garden, mounted the steps and rang the bell. Disconcertingly, the door was opened immediately by both Claude Chabrol and his wife; for a moment the three of us stood silent in the hall. As I had anticipated, the first thing she asked me was if she could offer me something to drink. Before I could answer, she added, with what struck me as characteristic decisiveness, '*Un jus de fruits, peut-être? Orange pressé – frais. Vous n'avez pas de choix, Monsieur.*' She vanished into a back room, from which came the noise of fresh oranges being pressed in an automatic juice-extractor, while her husband led me into the salon. A pleasant, unpretentious room, looking on to a large back garden: Japanese prints, four birds in a pretty cage, a great many books about Hollywood (*The Films of Carole Lombard . . . Greta Garbo . . . Marlene Dietrich*). A Siamese cat jumped on my lap and began to purr loudly. She came back with a brandy-glass full of orange juice for me, and a smaller one for herself. Chabrol tactfully left us alone. Her clothes (blue slacks and a pale yellow shirt) and the way she sat on the sofa had a ceremonial informality somehow typical of her style. The routine experience was reversed: I had expected to find an actress, and here I was, confronted by the image.

'The first thing I do when I get a new script is think of the clothes that the character should wear. One cannot decide precisely how one will play the role until the filming starts, as so much depends on the other actors. For instance Michel Bouquet, who played opposite me in *La Femme Infidèle* and *Juste*

Avant la Nuit, has taught me more about acting than anybody else: my performances took their tone from his. Jean Yanne, my leading man in *Le Boucher*, is a much more instinctive actor than Bouquet, less intellectual in his approach to the role, and so my acting in that film was different. Again, in *Les Noces Rouges*, Michel Piccoli has a totally different style from the others, and I adapted mine to his. So to start with I concentrate on the clothes, and through them I try to get inside the character. If you take care of the exterior, the interior follows. In a way the acting profession is a very moral one, because it forces one to control one's appearance. I believe that people's characters show on their faces. Sometimes you find an unpleasant person with a beautiful face – but that is a rare gift from heaven. I went to a concert given by Marlene Dietrich for charity – and some of the women in the audience, you could tell what they were like by their faces, terrible. Someone like Michèle Morgan is lucky: she has a lovely face and an amiable disposition. Others have to work at it. When I was very young I had difficulty getting on with people and it showed in my face. Now I find it easier and I believe that shows too.

'My favourite designer is Karl Lagerfeld, and he has taught me a lot about what to wear in films. The clothes must be fashionable, but not too fashionable, or they will date before the film comes out. In the Buñuel it was important to wear no loud colours, nothing too noticeable. And for the night scenes one had to wear something light, but Buñuel insisted that it should not be too light. It was complicated! That was one thing Buñuel told me: the other was "Don't think about anything at all." And he forbade the actresses to make up; we rehearsed, then shot the scene without a pause. But Delphine Seyrig, Bulle Ogier and I were meant to be bourgeoises – that was the whole point – and I suppose we *are* bourgeoises, so we were always secretly fixing our make-ups and hair-dos. Buñuel had a strange contraption like a periscope with which he used to spy on us and catch us out . . . In *Le Boucher* I made a mistake. The dress I wear in the first scene, the wedding party, is much too elegant. I'm supposed to be a provincial schoolmistress (though to make it easier we said that she had been born in Paris) and I tried very hard to suggest the provincial's idea of chic. But that first dress was all wrong. It's amusing – in *Les Noces Rouges* I have a foulard handbag from Hermès which I was very pleased with, it seemed exactly right for the character. But you never see it in the film! Only once, when the camera is behind me, it is just visible for a moment. Do please watch out for that moment when you see the film . . .

'Did you notice how I kept on changing my clothes throughout *Juste Avant la Nuit?* It seemed to me that the woman I played was so unbelievably bourgeoise that there was nothing else to do with her. That film took a vaudeville situation and treated it seriously. I didn't like being in it, and Bouquet was wrong for his part too. To cheer myself up, I insisted on riding my new motor-bike in the film. It's my latest passion . . . I have no favourite role, but I like one or two scenes in each film I make. For instance, the scene in the Buñuel when I invite the gardener to dinner – I was pleased with that. She treats him like a piece of furniture. But there are always weaknesses. Claude says, if there are *some* good moments, that's enough. And he taught me that there's no such thing as a small scene. As in real life, everything is equally important. One must get at the truth. When you act with a really good actor, everything becomes true. And if I've acted well with Claude it's because he's a good director, not because he's my husband. Sometimes his films are difficult to make convincing, but that is like life, where one never knows how others will react. You may know people very well, but often you are surprised. He likes scenes at table because he believes that then, with the family united, hidden tensions are revealed. Meals are formally dramatic.'

Stéphane Audran thinks that the Paris theatre is *moche*. She was offered the Vivien Merchant part in Pinter's *Old Times*, with Delphine Seyrig, but refused. 'That was before I became a friend of Delphine's, and when one doesn't know her she can be a bit overwhelming . . . The French production was terrible, nothing but pauses, I was well out of that.' She finds the acting profession, with its limited cast and endless theatrical gossip, depressingly parochial, and when she goes to the country to walk, swim or ski she loves meeting people who are outside it. 'I hate being bored, and with people I meet like that I am never bored. Also, one learns from them things that help one when judging a script. I understand Buñuel when he says that he doesn't like actors, he likes people. That is why he seems so young, like a child of ten. One feels much older than him, although he is such a great man. But my first day on his film wasn't easy. I had just had a row with the producer and I arrived late. I thought I had an hour to prepare, but I had to film at once. With Monsieur Buñuel, you have to enter his universe, and I was still in Chabrol's . . . '

Her friend Karl Lagerfeld is editing an issue of French *Vogue* devoted to Marlene Dietrich, who will allow only two other actresses to be included: Romy Schneider and Stéphane Audran. 'I was flattered, but surprised,' said the latter. 'She didn't think I was at all well dressed in the Buñuel and couldn't understand a word of the film. The only thing she liked me in was *Les Biches*. Poor Marlene, she is very lonely in Paris, so many of her friends are dead. I don't want to stay young forever, but it must be awful when one's friends die . . . Film acting is difficult. Like an athlete, one has to get into training. Some days one isn't on form. Great discipline is needed – but it is a good discipline. Marlene has it, of course. At the time of *Les Cousins* I was so lazy, I didn't reflect, I lived from day to day. One has to learn the discipline as one gets older. So many women who could be beautiful allow all their bad thoughts to be written on their faces.'

Stéphane Audran's future plans are vague. There is no part for her in her husband's latest film, which will deal with the priesthood, and she, anyhow, believes that for a while their careers should follow separate paths. 'We've done such an enormous amount together. We make each other nervous – he can't be the same with me as with other actors.' The thing she would like most of all is a part in the next film that Buñuel makes.

She was showing me old photographs of herself when Chabrol came back into the room and offered me a cigar. 'Darling,' she said, 'what was the name of that film I made with Claude Pinoteau?' '*Les Durs à Cuire*,' he replied. 'What a man! He knows everything,' she remarked, and I could not decide whether or not this flash of conjugal flirtatiousness was intended to be ironic. She told me how proud and pleased she had been made by a recent issue of *Elle* magazine, in which a hairdresser called Jean-Marc Maniatis ('He's the very best!') nominated her as the film-star most in the fashion. 'She takes her tone from the fashion and gives it hers,' he wrote. 'After the last Buñuel, in which I did her hair, nearly 200 women came to me asking for the same style.' The magazine also contains a drawing by her little boy, in which his parents are portrayed driven by a Negro chauffeur in an elaborately decorated Rolls-Royce. Monsieur is smoking a cigar; Madame looks hard and elegant; a flag with 'Chabrol' on it flies from the bonnet: the little sketch conjures up a fantasy of bourgeois opulence which amused and delighted its models.

The front-door bell rang, and Chabrol admitted a tall, grey-haired man. 'You've come at the right moment,' he told him, 'just in time for the cheesecake.' Perhaps I had been seeing too many Chabrol films, but I immediately had a vision of a succulent dish waiting in the kitchen, to be consumed by the three of them after my departure. If it *had* been a film, the triangular evening would very likely end in murder . . . Then it struck me that 'cheesecake' might have been meant to refer to the pictures of Stéphane Audran which still littered the dining table. It was clearly time for me to take my leave. While doing so, I said, with truth, that I had found the interview very interesting. 'Did she *really* say anything interesting?' Chabrol asked, in comic disbelief. 'Next time you come,' said Stéphane Audran, 'I shall be even more interesting, if that is possible. Next time you come, I shall tell you everything!'

1973

GLORIA GRAHAME

M OST MEN WHO WENT TO THE MOVIES DURING THE 1950S were a little bit in love with Gloria Grahame. She was too unusual, both in looks and talent, to become a household name, and there was never such a thing as a Gloria Grahame 'vehicle'. She might turn up in any film, good or bad, playing almost any part, large or small, and whenever she did the result was exciting. Her upper lip was too long for conventional beauty, but her provocative, humorous pout, combined with the cool gaze of her candidly delinquent eyes, released a powerful erotic charge beyond the range of many more celebrated sex symbols. Her performances were enthusiastically received by the critics; for her acting, like her appearance, had something slightly odd about it which produced a complex response of surprised recognition. Her style was individual without being eccentric; although her technique was admirably straightforward and clear-cut, she always seemed to be holding something back. These hints and suggestions never degenerated into a banal 'mystery'; yet somehow she made you wonder, somehow she kept you guessing.

I first became aware of her in 1950, when she played opposite Humphrey Bogart in Nicholas Ray's *In a Lonely Place*, though this was in fact her tenth film. (Her debut had been in *Blonde Fever*, six years earlier.) She made seventeen more films during that decade and then virtually disappeared from the cinema, confining her appearances to the American stage and television. One especially remembers her egging on Jack Palance to murder Joan Crawford in *Sudden Fear*; as a silly Southern belle in *The Bad and the Beautiful*; having scalding coffee thrown in her face in *The Big Heat*; as a witty Ado Annie in *Oklahoma!* and a devastating *femme fatale* in *Human Desire*.

I knew almost nothing about her private life, and the one fact to be widely reported in the press was, like her screen

68

personality, intriguingly off-beat. Her first husband was the director Nicholas Ray; after divorcing him she married a producer called Cy Howard. Then, after divorcing *him*, she married Nick Ray Jr, her former stepson, thus becoming in a fashion her own daughter-in-law. This news item made one reflect how excellent she might have been as Phaedra.

Earlier this year, Gloria Grahame came to England to play Sadie Thompson in a revival of *Rain* at Watford. The old Somerset Maugham melodrama is usually interpreted by actresses as an exercise in hysterical histrionics and an opportunity to dress up in a flamboyant assortment of bangles, boas and boots. She chose a more subtle approach; her performance was sensitive and subdued, almost self-effacing. 'I've met prostitutes in my life and I have never found them to be flashy or coming on strong,' she told an interviewer in *The American*. 'I wanted to show Sadie as a girl who was dressed beautifully but simply, because I don't think of her as having something to sell.' The audience and reviewers were somewhat puzzled by the production, but the comeback could be counted a success and led to an engagement in a new play called *A Tribute to Lili Lamont*. Rehearsals for this had not yet started when I arranged to meet her for lunch.

I was just setting out for Langan's Brasserie, in Mayfair, to keep my appointment with Gloria Grahame, when the telephone rang. 'Oh, thank God I found you! Listen, this is Gloria . . . ' In her seductive voice (breathy, broken, solemn yet somehow amused) she told me that a terrible thing had happened. All her money, her chequebook and her credit cards had been stolen. She didn't know what to do, she was in despair. I suggested that we put off our meeting. 'No, don't do that. Don't move, just stay by the phone, and I'll call you back. Right?' After half an hour, she rang again. She still sounded desperate, but her news was good: the missing articles had been found at the back of a drawer in her bedroom. 'But I'm in such a state, I just have to take a nice long shower. I'll never find Langan's – can I meet you in two hours' time at the subway station on Leye-sester Square? I can get there direct from Chalk Farm.' I offered to pick her up at her home in a taxi.

The door of the rented flat off Adelaide Road was opened by

a dignified, rather bent old lady, wearing black. She showed me into a sitting room and let it be known, without actually saying so, that she was Gloria's mother. They had been to Stratford the night before, to see *The Taming of the Shrew*, and she discussed a production of the play by Sir Frank Benson's touring company which she had seen many years ago and never forgotten. 'I'll just go and find out what's keeping Gloria.' Alone in the room, I noticed beside me a battered scrapbook of ancient press-cuttings. Rather guiltily, I opened it, and read about little Jeannie MacDougall, a child singer of Scottish ballads, who matured into Jean Grahame, Shakespearian actress (Celia and Olivia on the northern circuit) and ended up as Mrs Leslie Hallward, drama coach and director at the Pasadena Playhouse in California. Mrs Hallward came back, and caught me reading her notices. 'Don't tell Gloria I showed you these, whatever you do,' she said in a soft voice, which attractively combined the classic elocution of a RADA training with a faint Scots burr. We talked about the Edwardian theatre until Gloria appeared at last.

Taller than I had expected, and remarkably slim, she wore white jeans and a grey T-shirt; her hair was arranged in a funny fuzz of shiny rat's tails. 'I'm never late – never! Am I, Mother? Mother will tell you I'm just never late! But this terrible thing happened . . . And I've been so worried about my hair . . . '

In the taxi she swerved round on her seat to face me and fixed me with her intimate, challenging gaze. Her manner was at the same time confidential and vague; she seemed on the point of laughing (whether at me or with me hardly mattered); she made me feel we were out on a spree. She chattered on about Shakespeare and how she longed to play in him – any part, Lady Macbeth, Juliet, *any* part – how privileged she would be to act for the Royal Shakespeare Company – she would do it for nothing, just accept a walk-on role – whom should she ring up about it? I mentioned the name of Trevor Nunn, and she jotted it down in a notebook.

The restaurant had nearly finished serving lunch when we arrived there. Gloria ordered coffee. After that, she asked for shellfish, but there was none on the menu so she settled for a glass of milk. Later, she said she wanted to try the chocolate gateau; the kitchen was closed by now, but she eventually got it. 'I'm really having a good time,' she said. 'I just can't get over that you want to write about me. Whatever will you say?'

'Tell me about *Lili Lamont*.'

'It's about a movie star.'

'What kind of movie star?'

'Just a movie star, I guess. To tell you the truth, I read it some time ago and I've completely forgotten it! I suppose you think that's awful?'

What other parts would she like to play? 'Elvira in *Blithe Spirit* and Amanda in *Private Lives*. I'm really good at accents, you know.' She did a speech from *Private Lives* in faultless Coward English, then switched to Cockney followed by Scots.

Favourite film? '*Crossfire*. That was at the time of the McCarthy witch hunts and none of us got an Oscar though we should have.'

She began to rummage vaguely in her handbag, and suddenly produced her passport. 'Wouldn't it have been terrible if I'd lost this too? It wasn't among the things I thought had gone, but just think if it had been! You haven't asked me how old I am, you know. Well, there it is – documentary evidence!' Opposite 'date of birth' the year 1933 had been firmly printed. I was too tactful to blurt out that *Crossfire* had been made in 1947, and her role in it had not been that of a fourteen-year-old girl.

How did she begin? 'Well, Mother coached me in Shakespeare and I acted in school plays. When I was a Girl Scout I was in something called *The Princess Whose Pride was Broken*. Then I understudied thirteen women in San Francisco and Chicago and one day the ingenue didn't show up for the matinee. That led to New York. I understudied Miriam Hopkins in *The Skin of Our Teeth* for ages. I was playing a Scots barmaid for George Abbott in *Highland Fling* when Louis B. Mayer spotted me from the audience. I refused to take a screen test – didn't see much point – but he gave me a contract of 250 dollars week. Just at that time the Theatre Guild asked me to play Ann Boleyn opposite Charles Laughton, but I went off and did the silly little waitress in *Blonde Fever* instead. I never bother to watch my old films. It's too late to do anything about them now, isn't it? In the fall I'm going to make a movie in Costa Rica. It's called *The Emerald Clue* and it has a fabulous cast . . . Do you *really* want to hear all this? Listen, I've got to get to a place called Kensington. How will I find it?'

I took her in another taxi. 'Both my parents are British, though I was born in California. Have you ever heard of a book called *The Picture of Dorian Gray* by Oscar Wilde? You have? Well, it's all about my family. My father's father was a painter and a great friend of Oscar Wilde. He suggested the whole idea of the story to Wilde, about the picture ageing and the beautiful boy remaining young, so Wilde called the artist in the book Basil Hallward, which was my grandfather's name. My father was a writer once, he wrote plays for my mother, but after they married and moved to America he became an industrial designer. He was so sad to give up writing – but wait a minute, he didn't, he wrote a lovely book last year, it was a children's book, about this frog . . . What was it called? I can't remember the name. But it was about a frog.'

The taxi and I waited for some time outside a block of flats near Olympia. She finally emerged carrying about half a dozen bottles containing various liquids. 'Know what these are? *Dye!* That was my hairdresser in there, he's very special. Now why don't you leave me outside the subway on Leye-sester Square?'

I said I would take her home. Did she have any children? 'Yes, two sons, aged fifteen and twelve. They live with their father in Malibu. Let's play favourite movies. What's your very favourite movie? Sir Laurence Olivier in *Henry V*?' When we parted, she pursed her lips exaggeratedly, leant forward and kissed me on the mouth. 'Well, I couldn't go home and write an article about *you*. Or maybe I could . . . '

1978

BRANDO

T HE ART OF ACTING MAY BE SEEN AS RANGING BETWEEN TWO poles: that of the mimic and that of the star. One sinks himself in the part, the other absorbs the part into his own pervasive personality. But most good actors establish a position somewhere between these two extremes, combining in different proportions the faculty of external observation with that of imaginative interpretation. At his best, Marlon Brando can be placed bang in the middle, where the perfect compromise is reached: he is the part, and the part is him.

This actor's powers of mimicry have attracted less attention than his star quality. But they are phenomenal, enabling him to impersonate with distinction a range of characters that includes a Mexican revolutionary (*Viva Zapata*, 1952), Mark Antony (*Julius Caesar*, 1953), Napoleon (*Desirée*, 1954), a Broadway gambler (*Guys and Dolls*, 1955), a Japanese interpreter (*Teahouse of the August Moon*, 1956), a Nazi officer (*The Young Lions*, 1958), an upper-class English naval officer (*Mutiny on the Bounty*, 1962) and a stuffy American diplomat (*The Ugly American*, 1963). Yet, to his public, Brando is most closely associated with three more personal performances: Stanley Kowalski in *A Streetcar Named Desire*, which he created on the New York stage in 1947 and filmed four years later; the neo-Fascist thug in *The Wild One* (1954); and the abused but dumbly triumphant martyr-hero of *On the Waterfront*, made the same year. The first two roles, at least, were very different from his own character (he is a gentle, introspective man with liberal sentiments), but his playing of them released an extraordinary power which established him as a symbol of the decade, perhaps the first anti-hero to operate within a popular medium. His good looks, and some quality within him that is insuperably sympathetic, may have muddled the ethical issues: the thug in *The Wild One* was more glorified than condemned, and it was possible to accept *Streetcar* as the story of a healthy young man plagued by a tiresome sister-in-law. A star performance often contradicts the script, and here Brando's talent for impersonation was outstripped by his compulsion towards self-expression. As a result, he became the mythic archetype of the violent, confused, anti-social element celebrated in American art throughout the 1950s. It was his successor, and persistent imitator, the late James Dean, who starred in *Rebel Without a Cause*; but the phrase might have been coined for Brando.

In *On the Waterfront*, however, the hero was supposed to *have* a cause. Here the streak of masochism in Brando's art reached the surface. Surely the hero was taking a little more punishment than was strictly necessary? His glamour began to acquire the morbid allure associated with portraits of Saint Sebastian. Instead of the arrows still quivering in the marshmallow flesh we had the bruised but beautiful boy, the broken boxer's nose, the exalted, inarticulate propensity for pain. The public cause (something about union dues and waterfront protection gangs) was forgotten in a private apotheosis.

As Brando followed *On the Waterfront* with more extrovert performances, it seemed possible at the time that this masochistic strain had been discovered and exploited by Kazan and did not necessarily typify the actor. After *Teahouse of the August Moon* he became sidetracked by the fashionable American cult of Japan (defeated nations exert a guilty fascination over their conquerors, so perhaps there was a touch of masochism here too), which resulted in *Sayonara*, one of his feeblest vehicles. But with the Western *One-Eyed Jacks*, released in 1961 after years of expensive preparation, it became clear that masochism was a central motivation.

This was a one-man show: Brando directed himself, and personally supervised the script and details of production. Here was an artist publicly and painstakingly acting out his own fantasies, his own romantic view of his potentialities and limitations. These took the form of repeated humiliations, culminating in a long, slow whipping scene treated with the ritual solemnity of a holy flagellation. Similarly, his unsentimental and well-observed performance in *Mutiny on the Bounty* reached its climax in a painfully mawkish death scene, for which it is likely that Brando himself was responsible.

It is significant that, when given (or, anyway, taking) his head (in *The Chase*), he chose a Western. For there is something juvenile, touchingly immature, about his personality on the screen. Most actors are self-centred – they have to be; but Brando's egotism has a quality of bewildered introspection peculiar to adolescence. Perhaps even the mimicry can be seen as the parrot-like precocity of an observant child. The success of Salinger's *The Catcher in the Rye* had established the suffering, inarticulate teenager with a ferocious eye for phoniness and, as it were, set the cultural scene for Brando's tentative mumble and *gauche* grace. His star quality was rooted in the contemporary concept of adolescent sanctity: was he perhaps the original 'crazy mixed-up kid'?

Throughout the 1950s Brando was relentlessly copied. It is possible that, as the most illustrious Old Boy of the Actors' Studio of New York, he may even have influenced the later style of Marilyn Monroe, the only other film star with whom he can be compared. Both have brilliantly explored the excitement of the defenceless mind. But if Brando, like all great stars, has a bisexual appeal, this has nothing to do with effeminacy. It is rather the androgynous uncertainty that often accompanies the age of puberty, when sensibilities are intensified by physical ambiguity.

Brando's acting has the poetry of free assocation in that state of mind between sleeping and waking, at the same time clear and confused. He moves at a different pace to his colleagues – the pace of a semi-somnambulist. And, as it is said that sleepwalkers instinctively avoid bumping into furniture or falling out of windows, so Brando never comes to grief. The intellect is dulled, but something else takes control – some uncomplicated emotional response, linked to pre-natal memory, infantile and innocent. This preserves him from accident, steering him past the technical traps and vulgar errors into which all but the most polished professionals must sometimes fall.

Since Brando's first film in 1950, the course of American

acting, as if under deep analysis, began a regressive journey back to the womb. On the way, it uncovered many beauties and insights that had never been expressed in this medium before. But it remains a backward journey, becoming less interesting as it nears its goal; for beyond the womb there is nothing – 'In my beginning is my end'. For the past few years, Brando has been active, but with the exercise of marking time. The hips thicken, the hair thins, but the adolescent beauty remains: it is a question of temperament rather than age.

Like all stars intimately identified with a particular period, he has dated early – but in the way that a classic dates. Seeing his recent films, seeing again his old ones, it is possible to feel some impatience with his private style, that air of knowing a sad secret that never can be told. We think we have guessed the secret, and may wish that he had developed even further his gift for objective characterisation; but the gift would wither without the nourishment of his extravagant subjectivity. He's stuck with his image; to deny it now would be to deny himself.

1966

ALICE FAYE: PORTRAIT OF A HEROINE

(A talk delivered at the Institute of Contemporary Arts as part of a Symposium of Heroines)

BEFORE MAKING A CLAIM FOR ALICE FAYE AS A REPRESENTATIVE type of film heroine, I should explain that I use the word 'heroine' in a limited sense. There was nothing heroic about the roles she played and she never suggested personal heroic qualities as did Joan Crawford, Barbara Stanwyck, Judy Garland, Ingrid Bergman and Anna Magnani; she did not go in for being larger than life, she was far from the *monstre sacrée*. But she was a perfect heroine if the word is taken to mean the feminine complement to the hero; she played a passive, placid, mainly decorative part, and succeeded, in my opinion, beyond any other actress of her generation in conveying sweetness without being at all insipid. Although for a period she represented on the screen the blonde ideal, she was seldom brassy and suggested neither the gold-digger (with all those stale jokes about sugar-daddies, diamonds and mink coats) nor the good pal; and while she never played intellectual roles, she scorned, thank goodness, the idea of guying herself as a dumb blonde. Her blondeness dated back to the serious, innocent type first exemplified on the screen by Mary Pickford, long before Jean Harlow introduced the conception of cheerful amorality, the tough baby who drinks glass for glass with her man and has a good heart underneath. One aspect of the Harlow type soon became embalmed in the aunt-like figure of Eve Arden, with her wry, reassuring jokes against herself; another blossomed into baroque extravagance with Mae West. Variations of the main tradition persist until today; for a while it was maintained,

77

in a very watered-down version, by Betty Grable, and echoes of it are to be heard in the excellent performances of Judy Holliday and Marilyn Monroe. But Alice Faye has no worthy successor. When she retired from the screen her place was filled for a short time by June Haver, who proved a very unsatisfactory understudy; after June Haver took the veil, the heroines of American musicals tended to be piquante, athletic ex-teenagers like Mitzi Gaynor and Debbie Reynolds, or frankly eccentric specialists like Esther Williams with her underwater ballet and Kathryn Grayson with her strained coloratura.

Alice Faye was born in New York in 1915, the daughter, I believe, of a policeman. At an early age she drew attention to herself singing with Rudy Vallee's band, and under Vallee's auspices she made her film debut in *George White's Scandals of 1934*. This was also the year that Betty Grable made her first screen appearance, singing 'Knock Knees' with Edward Everett Horton in *The Gay Divorcee*. For ten years Alice Faye reigned supreme as leading lady in the Twentieth Century Fox musicals, making thirty-two films before her retirement at the early age of thirty. At first she played second leads (in 1936 she twice supported Shirley Temple, in *Poor Little Rich Girl* and *Stowaway*); then the following year she stole *On the Avenue* from Madeleine Carroll and became a star in her own right. Perhaps the peak of her career was reached in 1938, when she teamed up with Tyrone Power and Don Ameche to form an unforgettable triangle in *Alexander's Ragtime Band* and *In Old Chicago*.

At the beginning of the war, however, a subtle change in public taste could be discerned; Alice Faye's gentle, relaxed personality, chocolate-box prettiness and low, caressing voice still had their admirers, but the times demanded something rather livelier. In 1940 she starred in a film called *Tin Pan Alley* with John Payne, Jack Oakie – and Betty Grable. Grable had been doing soubrette roles all this time, and her part in *Tin Pan Alley* was similar to Faye's in *On the Avenue* – that is to say, it had a touch of 'character' about it. Grable seized her chance, and soon shot ahead to become the GI's favourite pin-up girl. Alice Faye made several more films, in two of which attention was distracted from her by the presence of Carmen Miranda; but she only came into her own again in 1943, with *Hello, Frisco,*

Hello and *The Gang's All Here* (known in England as *The Girls He Left Behind*). These films were in Technicolor, and Faye had never looked more spectacular; also, they each contained a number ('You'll Never Know' and 'No Love, No Nothing') which became as widely popular as such early Faye classics as 'Goodnight, My Love' from *Stowaway* and 'This Year's Kisses' from *On the Avenue*. However, Alice Faye, who was now divorced from Tony Martin and married to Phil Harris, retired from films, leaving the field clear for Grable. She made one last and ill-advised appearance in 1945 – in *Fallen Angel*, a sexy murder drama, where the bad-girl role was given to Linda Darnell and Alice Faye was ridiculously miscast as a frumpish spinster who plays the organ in church.

Alice Faye owed her peculiar charm to three factors: her looks, her singing voice, and her personality. Her singing was both attractive and effective, in an unsophisticated way; her voice was unusually low, and her style derived from the simplified 'torch' of the early 1930s, a style epitomised in the work of Ruth Etting, who recorded many of the numbers that Faye introduced. In appearance, Alice Faye was extremely pretty, with a touch of eccentricity in her beauty that inspired imitation while making it impossible to achieve. Her hair was a buttercup yellow – in some Technicolor films its colour reminded one of an advertisement for custard. One of her eyebrows was slightly slanted; her upper lip was rather long, and she had a trick, while singing, of pulling down her lower lip, which gave her face a rueful expression, as though she was depressed but amused at herself for being so. Her bosom was on the large side – in fact, apart from Ann Sheridan's, it was probably the biggest in the business until Jane Russell extended the standard size. Her legs were long and shapely; they seemed to start higher up in her body than is usually the case. As a whole her appearance combined coarseness and delicacy in a very attractive way; her large mouth, thick shining hair and prominent breasts were enhanced by her slender wrists and ankles, her dainty hands and feet, her gentle, friendly voice which suggested a compliant and rather helpless character. This placid, womanly, old-fashioned quality in her personality made a fascinating contrast to the sophisticated, chromium surface that covered it in her thirties films. It also enabled her to shine in those set in the vaguely *fin de siècle* era of which the makers of musicals used to be so fond; in *Lilian Russell, Hello, Frisco, Hello* and *In Old Chicago*, decked out in period costume, she achieved the dateless prettiness of the picture postcard and the biscuit box, which we associate with crinolines, greyhounds and weeping willows, with violets and Merry Widow hats. However, the old-fashioned element in her make-up should not be over-emphasised, for she was very much a contemporary type; she always suggested the prettiest girl in a Ziegfeld Follies chorus line. She made an ideal mannequin for the fashions of the thirties – white furs suited her particularly well – and an even better one for those of the war, the long bob, wedge-heeled shoes, broad shoulders and short skirt. She could easily have taken the romantic New Look in her stride, but she would never have survived the Audrey Hepburn age: ballet shoes, ponytails and jeans are enemies to everything she stood for.

It is difficult to know whether or not she was a good actress, for she seldom tried to act; she was above it. Even her singing owes part of its haunting appeal to her refusal to force any interpretation; there she stood, looking lovely, sang her song more or less straight, then stopped. In some scenes where she is a bystander one can almost see her attention wander; she sits at the edge of the screen, eating chocolate, obediently waiting for her cue. The dramatic scenes she was called upon to play were never very taxing; as a rule they consisted of tears because her song-writing lover had either allowed a rival to sing her favourite number, or had forced her to plug it in a nightclub when she had been looking forward to a cosy evening's rest from singing. In *Alexander's Ragtime Band* she is supposed to start as a vulgar floozie and, under Power's Pygmalion-like influence, grow gradually more ladylike as the film progresses; she makes the distinction adequately, but with an abruptness lacking in subtlety. She looked too luscious to convince as the spinster in *Fallen Angel*; in *Little Old New York* she made a hash of a comic role; and I remember an odd film called *Tail Spin*, in which she and Constance Bennett were teamed as heroic women aviators, and which only came to life when Alice Faye, between flights, sang 'Are You in the Mood for Mischief?' She could, however, rise to a moving occasion in her own way; as in *Rose of Washington Square*, when Tyrone Power escapes from gaol and arrives, unshaven and haggard, in the gallery of the theatre where she works, and sees the curtains part to reveal her, wearing a beret and a black satin skirt with a slit up the side, standing beneath a lamp-post and singing 'My Man'. Her rendering of 'This Year's Kisses' in *On the Avenue*, ignored during a rehearsal, is also remarkably poignant. But on the whole she transcended drama; she was there purely for entertainment. She was a true star in that her films needed no plot, no characterisation, no lavish production numbers; any leading man, any supporting cast, any old decor would do; give her a few good songs, a new vehicle as exactly like her old ones as possible, dress her up and put her in front of the camera and let her work her magic: her audience knew just what to expect, and knew that they were going to enjoy it.

1955

STREAM OF
SELF-CONSCIOUSNESS

T HE CINEMA, THAT PRECOCIOUS ART, HAS ENTERED A PHASE OF
self-consciousness which is threatening to stunt its
growth.

This is not to announce that it has passed from a primitive
stage of artless charm to one of technical sophistication and
aesthetic responsibility: it made *that* transition very early on in
its development – certainly before 1921, the year of Chaplin's *The
Kid*, Stroheim's *Foolish Wives*, Rex Ingram's *The Four Horsemen of
the Apocalypse*, Fritz Lang's *Destiny* and D. W. Griffith's *Orphans
of the Storm*. These directors already understood the medium to
be as complex, as demanding and potentially as powerful as
any other; they were self-conscious to the degree that (as art
involves self-expression) every artist must be conscious of himself. But the new self-consciousness is altogether different. It
contains an element of apology, of deprecation, which merges
into defiance and leads to a fatal self-indulgence. Films now
hysterically draw attention to the fact that they *are* films, as if
that were the point and everything else (visual beauty, intellectual content, even entertainment value) merely a pretext for
driving it home.

By a historical accident, the cinema came into being at a
moment when art in general was entering a self-conscious
phase – when writers were trying to transcend the limitations
of language and painters to redefine the function of paint. But,
in a self-consciously 'modern' age, the cinema had the great
advantage of *being* modern; a child of the twentieth century,
every move it made, whether good or bad, could only be
new. Without a history, it had no need to make a self-conscious rejection of the past: happily engaged in exploring its
own technical resources, it was spared the self-conscious

re-examination of tools (words, notes, perspectives) grown rusty with use in fabricating former masterpieces. Inevitably, it reflected some of the experiments and discoveries in other contemporary spheres: expressionism in *Caligari*, surrealism in Cocteau, popular Freud in a million middlebrow flashbacks. But, until recently, it has been too busy establishing itself to question or defend its right to exist. It has taken itself for granted. Now it is beginning to doubt its own identity, which it feels the need to assert by repeated allusions to its brief past. It has become a vehicle for its own reassurance.

There are two kinds of self-consciousness; the adolescent, betraying itself by painful shyness, *gauche* aggression or sulky silence; and the decadent, in which a mode of expression (clothes, speech, manners, style) is given an importance disproportionate to the thing expressed. The prototype for the first is the Bohemian and the prototype for the second is the Dandy: variations on these self-conscious figures recur throughout social history and the history of art. In the cinema, highbrow self-consciousness (mainly found in the work of French directors) is decadent in origin; lowbrow self-consciousness (the Bond films; *Whatever Happened to Baby Jane?*) is adolescent; middlebrow self-consciousness (*Tom Jones; A Hard Day's Night*) is a mixture of both. The key to all three is in the popular phrase – always spoken with approval – 'sending oneself up'.

Neither 'art' nor 'entertainment' can now be taken straight. Jean-Luc Godard, one of the most serious film-makers there has ever been, goes to desperate lengths to avoid a serious air and to deny a serious intention (with the ironic results that he sometimes succeeds too well). The James Bond films are shy of even the relative seriousness of the Fleming books, doggedly sending up a send-up. To appreciate *From Russia With Love* it is necessary to take the visual allusion to *Call Me Bwana*, made by the same company. Similarly, in *The Ipcress File* one is expected to recognise Len Deighton's cookstrip in Harry Palmer's kitchen. These films are embarrassed by the fact of being thrillers, which they successfully disguise beneath gossipy references and a mannered technique self-consciously aping thrillers of the past. But the results are less authentic, and much more pretentious, than the original models.

This embarrassment is a sign of immaturity, suggesting the careful *insouciance* and involuntary pomposity of a schoolboy's essay. If the cinema is too old to justify these adolescent contortions, it is not sufficiently ancient to excuse the Byzantine decadence into which its *avant-garde* is leading it. When we don't feel like reading a *nouveau roman*, we can turn back to the novels of Flaubert, Tolstoy, Dickens, Proust. Serious films today tend to concentrate, with an incestuous cannibalism, on purely cinematic material – endlessly celebrating, in self-consciously affectionate satire, a medium which has produced too few masterpieces to justify this narcissistic obsession.

When did the cinema get self-conscious? From the start of the star system it had featured individual performers who were prepared to caricature themselves (Mae West, Marlene Dietrich), and by the 1940s the tradition of the public private joke was well established – references to the skinniness of Frank Sinatra, the supposed rivalry between Bing Crosby and Bob Hope, the fact that Betty Grable was married to Harry James, and so on. But this was merely another device to accelerate Hollywood's machine for the manufacture of personalities, in which films themselves were cleverly exploited as a medium for their own publicity. I would guess that the first really self-conscious film – the first to send itself up as a whole – was John Huston's *Beat the Devil* (1953). Here the cast, which included such myth-makers as Humphrey Bogart, Peter Lorre, and Gina Lollobrigida, were invited to trade on their own screen histories, and the plot (a fantastic story of adventure and intrigue) took second place to incidental whimsy. Like so many of its successors, the film was vaguely supposed to incorporate satire on other films – in this case, Huston's own.

In the same year, Jacques Tati made *Les Vacances de Monsieur Hulot* – not in itself a self-conscious film, but one whose popularity indicated a growing self-consciousness in the climate of the cinema. Tati's style was connected with a facetious nostalgia for silent films on the part of the moviegoing public – for the

Keystone Kops in a speeded-up car chase, Pearl White pinioned to the railroad track, the bathetic charm of narrative subtitles. This is a self-conscious taste because it is ambiguous: it acknowledges the silent comedian to be genuinely funny, at the same time mocking the unintentional absurdity of silent-film technique. (Similarly, the 'camp' taste for Bette Davis and Joan Crawford finds their vehicles ridiculous yet recognises a real power in the personalities of the stars. For many years these ladies, playing straight, satisfied a diminishing public of matrons and homosexuals. Then, suddenly growing self-conscious themselves, they made *Baby Jane* and its horror-comic successors – which brought them a lot of money and almost as large a following as they had in their heyday. Self-consciousness had become necessary for survival.)

The facetious nostalgia for Keystone Kop whimsy was temporarily sidetracked on to the cinema's periphery: it was to be found in those arch foreign experimental cartoons that precede the main feature at 'art' movie houses, in television commercials, in the zany humour of the radio Goons and on the revue stage. It was not till 1959 that the first great self-conscious film was made; Godard's *A Bout de Souffle*. Now the built-in references were sophisticated rather than facetious, revealing rather than coy; and, instead of to the conventions of silent farce, they were to the sinister elegance of Hollywood gangster films as personified by Humphrey Bogart. Godard had made a serious *Beat the Devil*.

The next year, 1960, saw the flowering of highbrow self-consciousness in *Tirez sur le Pianiste* by Truffaut (whose earlier *Les Quatre Cent Coups* had been hardly self-conscious at all); in Malle's *Zazie dans le Métro*, perhaps the most self-conscious film ever made; in Demy's *Lola* with its hidden clues to its own construction and its deliberate sentimentality. Meanwhile, less gifted French directors were preparing to indulge in an orgy of self-consciousness with such films as *Dragées au Poivre* and *La Poupée*; and in America and England, whenever a group of young people banded together to make a low-budget 'experimental' film, the result was likely to be a send-up of other movies (*Hallelujah the Hills*) or an elaborately zany exploitation of early cinematic technique (*The Running, Jumping, and Standing Still Film*).

In 1963, the cinema of self-consciousness entered a new phase through the accident of *Tom Jones*. Coterie tricks of the highbrow cinema (facetious credits, fancy wipes, fast motion, sophisticated anachronisms) were given a lowbrow gloss to produce a middle-brow money-maker which (to the amazement of Woodfall itself) pleased both critics and the box-office. This film was first intended to strike a robust, authentically eighteenth-century note. Uncertain as to whether they had succeeded in this, its makers added some fashionable modern gimmicks and resigned themselves to failure. They were in for a pleasant surprise. Scenting a private joke, the public wished to be in on it and found, with relief, that it was easy to understand – not so very different, after all, from straightforward slapstick, yet dignified by the names of Henry Fielding and John Osborne among the credits. Tony Richardson had made a popular *Beat the Devil*.

Since the success of *Tom Jones* self-conscious films – once a diverting rarity – have become the depressing norm. Comedies, thrillers, musicals, dramas – all seem uneasily aware of some inherent absurdity within these categories; in an attempt to forestall criticism, they acknowledge this in advance. But banality cannot be avoided merely by calling attention to it. In his script for *Mata Hari* Truffaut included passages of dialogue from *Shanghai Express*, *Les Parapluies de Cherbourg*, *La Grande Illusion*, his own *Jules et Jim*, and no doubt from other films; then sat back and waited to see how many critics spotted the allusions. The critics, unnerved, now spot allusions that don't exist; this was shown by their reaction in England to Demy's beautiful *La Baie des Anges*. Unable to believe that this was as simple and straightforward as it seemed, they praised Jeanne Moreau's performance as a clever pastiche of some dizzy blonde from a crazy comedy of the 1930s – while in fact the character she created existed in its own right, with reference to the film that contained it and no other.

In some cases, self-consciousness may be justified as the best method of achieving originality – as in Dick Lester's *A Hard Day's Night*, which rightly encouraged the Beatles to 'be themselves'. For the Beatles, as for the Royal Family, a certain degree of self-consciousness is inevitable; they are personalities, independently of their function as performers.

But more often self-consciousness is allowed to run riot without reason or excuse. Clive Donner's *What's New Pussycat?* is a convenient (but by no means unique) example, actually containing within itself several varieties of current self-consciousness. These include New York Jewish sick humour (Woody Allen making jokes about sex, psychiatrists and being small); kooky comedy (Paula Prentiss making jokes about being tall); Goonish whimsy (the opening camera tricks, the presence of Peter Sellers); facetiously surrealist farce (Ursula Andress descending by parachute, a fat woman dressed as a Wagnerian soprano); and the ubiquitous cinematic in-joke (a send-up of Fellini's *8½*, itself an agonisingly self-conscious film of a more serious kind).

The self-conscious treatment of sex – exaggerated in *What's New Pussycat?* but to some degree present in most films today – is in effect oddly asexual and seldom really funny. It is based on words like 'kinky' and 'kooky' which, once they are used self-consciously, lose their original meaning and are degraded to stylised show-business clichés. Again and again one hears with misgiving of some new film that is really way-out, or kinky, or sick, that 'goes further than anything has before'. It is only right that film-makers should want to go as far as possible – but not, surely, in a direction so heavily signposted that it can only lead back to where they began. Louis Malle has been directing Brigitte Bardot and Jeanne Moreau in a film of which the main point seems to be that they are in it. This might have been an innocent continuation of the 'star vehicle' tradition, but in a self-conscious age it has to be presented as a pastiche of that tradition, the star vehicle to end them all.

Malle is, in fact, a key figure in the self-conscious movement. When he decided to film Raymond Queneau's *Zazie* he was faced with a highly sophisticated *tour de force* written in an invented language full of literary allusions and verbal puns. These he tried to replace by cinematic allusions and visual puns. His film had a delayed influence and the result has been, not a new film language, but a debasement of the old, which was insufficiently developed to stand the strain. Now cinematic allusions can take the place of direct observation, visual puns of psychological analysis (in Godard) or narrative tension (in Bond). Too often, the self-conscious cinema suggests an attempt to rewrite *Finnegans Wake* in Esperanto.

1965

In Defence Of Cinema Art

IN HIS ARTICLE 'PRIESTS OF THE HIGHBROW CINEMA', PUBLISHED in the January issue of *Encounter*, Nicola Chiaromonte accuses what he calls 'intellectualistic' film directors of attempting to use cinematic images as if they were words 'pregnant with profound, if vague, meanings instead of employing them to create the illusion of a real event'. 'There is no escape,' he writes, 'from the essential simple-mindedness of the movies.' This patronising attitude is itself an 'intellectualistic' platitude: the don who only likes Westerns and wouldn't be seen dead at a 'foreign' film is in England a familiar (if somewhat dated) figure. The implication is that the cinema should keep its place as an elementary, even primitive art form, fit only to purvey factual information or entertainment of an undemanding and relaxing kind; that it should not try to ape its betters by hoping 'to express ideological or lyrical meaning'. Of course Chiaromonte is right when he suggests that a film which tries *literally* to be a poem or an intellectual discourse is undertaking a hopeless task, just as a novel can never achieve the effect of music; but he is wrong to assume that the 'priests of the highbrow cinema' are necessarily aiming at results already patented by other forms of art. What they are trying to do (with varying degrees of success) is to define and explore the potentialities peculiar to films. These have only recently been acknowledged, but there is no reason why they should not be as great as those of any other medium for artistic expression.

Chiaromonte opens his article with the words: 'A footprint on the sand is the *sign* of a man's passage. The cross is the *symbol* of Christianity.' Here he seems to refute his own argument in advance, for the cross is an *image*, the visual presentation of which in various contexts can convey as many subtle shades of meaning as the use of the word 'cross' in a poem. It has often been successfully exploited in films to achieve emotional and intellectual overtones: a famous example was the flick-knife disguised as a crucifix in Buñuel's *Viridiana*. He goes on:

> A word is a sign only when it is used in a strictly utilitarian way – to indicate or command. In other cases words, even though they have a precise meaning, change with their context . . . A word, then, can be a symbol. A photograph, however, can only be a sign, an unequivocal sign of the passage of a material object before the camera-eye.

This is unconvincing; there is nothing unequivocal about a photograph. Simple proof of this was unintentionally provided on television not long ago, when two different programmes on the same day used identical sequences from newsreels of World War I. In one, musical accompaniment and commentary succeeded in producing an uplifting and patriotic effect; in the other, the effect was exactly the opposite – a bitter indictment of the horror of war.

Movies are created, not in the studio or on location, but in the cutting-room. Photographs are the director's raw material. When he edits these – cutting up strips of celluloid and piecing them together again – he has the same chance of creating a work of art as the writer has when he organises words on the page, the painter when he applies his brush to the canvas, the composer when he exploits the resources of musical instruments. Any 'still' from his film can be modified or transformed by the images that precede and succeed it in the same way that a word, a brush-stroke, a note in music are dependent on context for significance. In practice, of course, most directors do not take this opportunity, but edit their films along conventional lines, to produce more or less adequate additions to the entertainment industry. (Directors have often been prevented from editing their own films by the studios.) But the great directors have always ignored conventions, or adapted them to their own, original uses.

To illustrate his highly debatable point that a succession of photographic images can only be an objective *sign*, never a subjective *symbol*, Chiaromonte writes:

All we have to do is to see a film twenty years old to realise how ephemeral the cinematic medium is. The movies, which at first glance seem to speak the most realistic and unequivocal language, quickly become stiff, mannered, and unreal.

It is true that most films date very quickly (though not much faster than second-rate painting and literature), but this applies only to conventional products, depending for their popularity on a formula, a topical plot, or a favourite star. As fashions in story-telling alter these naturally become quaint (and often increasingly attractive as a result). The elements that date them are the women's clothes, the received ideas of morality, the standards for glamour current at their period: they are *intended* as ephemera, and the passage of time gives them the academic interest of social history. But the good 'art films' never date. *L'Atalante, Ivan the Terrible, L'Age D'Or* are stylised, self-conscious works of art, expressing in a pure form the genius of their creators, and they transcend the narrative limitations which Chiaromonte would like to impose on the cinema as a whole. It is hard to explain their survival, for the language of film criticism still lags behind its subject. One can compare Vigo's film to a lyrical poem, Eisenstein's to a Byzantine church, Buñuel's to an anarchist manifesto: but in doing so one is borrowing terms from other spheres of artistic activity and therefore confusing the issue. One is making the mistake of which Chiaromonte accuses Resnais, Antonioni and Bergman – a mistake of which they are not all, and not always, guilty.

The fact that these three widely different directors should have been lumped together in his article shows that Chiaromonte is in some confusion about the cinema; he here makes an error typical of the philistine who assumes that the objects of his resentment must have other things in common beyond the fact that he cannot understand them. Many of his strictures do, in fact, apply to Resnais' *L'Année Dernière à Marienbad*, an arty and pretentious work which has inspired the same kind of fashionable enthusiasm and meaningless debate as Rutland Boughton's *The Immortal Hour*, Barrie's *Mary Rose*, or some

Victorian academic 'problem picture'. By deliberately withholding significance from the images they present on the screen and giving the audience *carte blanche* as regards interpretation, Resnais and Robbe-Grillet provide ammunition for the philistine argument that images arranged in an unconventional sequence *cannot* have significance. Ingmar Bergman, on the other hand, is an entirely conventional director, who makes fairly straightforward 'literary' films, occasionally decorated by a baroque or Gothic-revival extravagance borrowed from the expressionist theatre. The only genuine innovator mentioned by Chiaromonte is Antonioni, whose films appear slow-moving to some people because he adjusts the balance of narrative technique to give internal and external development equal weight. He is one of the most acute analysts of social behaviour and psychological tension that the cinema has ever known, but the indisputable accuracy of his social observation is ignored by his detractors, who are affronted by his subtle exploration of psychological conditions. ' . . . An empty street,' Chiaromonte complains,

> which is supposed to indicate (who knows how or why) the state of mind of a character – to say nothing of the ideas of the director – is simply a static image. It indicates nothing. The picture of an empty street can be superb as photography, but it is only the picture of an empty street.

Antonioni's films are full of empty streets, deserted crossroads, blank walls, long passages: these belong to his narrative style, and in the hands of imitators (as, for example, Patroni Griffi with *Il Mare*) are in danger of becoming clichés. But every artistic innovator creates new clichés. In an Antonioni film, emotional meaning is allowed to accrue round inanimate objects as it does in life. A place seen for the first time makes an impression that is unrecognisable later, when it has become familiar. The island in *L'Avventura* changes from a romantic pleasure-ground into a forbidding, desolate waste, because of what has happened on it – but the change is subjective, not physical. The least successful scene in *La Notte* is the climax, when the wife reads the husband's love-letter aloud and he fails to recognise it. Here,

Antonioni is making words do what he has already done, as precisely if more suggestively, with images of emptiness.

Chiaromonte writes as if the 'priests of the highbrow cinema' were a new phenomenon, mentioning only three comparatively young men. He says nothing of Eisenstein, Vigo, Renoir, Welles; and nothing of Truffaut and Godard who are making experiments with editing as daring as Antonioni's, and by deliberate allusions to the golden age of Hollywood incorporate and intellectualise (very French, this) some of the mindless glamour belonging to the commercial cinema at its most ephemeral. While the Italian's experiments give a superficial impression of ponderous slowness, those of the young French directors given an equally misleading impression of flippancy and speed. Why should we accept the arbitrary treatment of time adopted by the conventional cinema, and borrowed from conventional novels and plays? Films can approach nearer to the immediacy of human experience than any other medium. They can show that the passage of time is subjective; that a short walk to the bus-stop can seem to last an age, while the long bus journey can apparently pass in a second; that our apprehension of reality can be modified by memories (perhaps distorted) of the past and by vague prophecies of the future. Antonioni expands time; Godard contracts it; Resnais reorganises it; Agnès Varda, in *Cleo de 5 à 7*, scrupulously preserves it.

Chiaromonte acknowledges that

> The resources of the cinema are enormously rich. It has at its disposal a realm where all is explicit and accessible, where act immediately follows on intention, and where real life is magically transformed into a series of clear and definite events. But it is certainly not through the cinema that we can explore what Heraclitus called 'the confines of the soul'.

Why not? In a sense, all art clarifies: when the cinema is vague to no purpose, ambiguous for the sake of ambiguity, it is neither better nor worse than a pretentious poem or play. But to insist that the cinema must limit itself to the portrayal of 'a series of clear and definite events' is to claim that painting should have remained representational, that the theatre should observe the classical unities, that verse should never be 'free'. It is confining the medium to the nickelodeon; halting its development at *The Great Train Robbery*, where it began; denying its unique and obvious opportunities for the effortless mingling of objective accuracy with subjective interpretation. It is because the cinema's technical resources for matching the surface of life are so rich, and have as yet been so little exploited, that a film director of genius today is in a stronger position than any other modern artist to penetrate beneath the surface and reach 'what Heraclitus called "the confines of the soul" '.

1963

DIARY

AT A FRIEND'S HOUSE, I SAW A VIDEO OF *LIEBELEI*, MAX OPHULS'S beautiful film of Arthur Schnitzler's play which was shown on television some months ago. Made in 1932, this masterpiece is a rarity: although the Third Reich censors removed Ophuls's name from the credits and he left Germany on the day after the Reichstag fire, it was banned by the Allied Commission when the war was over because its success had happened to coincide with the Nazi regime. It begins behind the scenes at the Vienna Opera House. The first act of *The Abduction from the Seraglio* has just ended; the stage-manager anxiously looks out through a peephole in the curtain to survey the crowded stalls and balconies. We share his view – the spectators are now being spied on. Then, the chandelier in the auditorium flares alight to herald the arrival of the Emperor; the audience rise, turn their backs on the stage and gaze up at the Royal Box. Very subtly – almost subliminally – Ophuls has adumbrated a mystery central to drama: who is being watched, and by whom?

Went to a matinée of *Re: Joyce!*, Maureen Lipman's brilliant impersonation of Joyce Grenfell at the Fortune Theatre. An odd experience. Grenfell, whose solo performances were based on the accurate re-creation of closely observed social mannerisms, is herself closely observed and accurately re-created by Lipman. The audience applauded every item with increasing enthusiasm, ending in a wild ovation – for whom? For Grenfell or for Lipman? Some of them may not have been quite sure. This element of doubt in their delight is typical of that teasing ambiguity which has always been inherent in the act of theatregoing – an ambiguity exploited to fullest effect by the art of Barry Humphries.

Perhaps because I have spent so much time over so many years watching television at home, the art of theatregoing now

95

strikes me as more than ever peculiar, almost a little crazy – an excitingly ancient anachronism and an undertaking fraught with risk. It seems so perverse, somehow, to find oneself in the same room as the actors (for even in the cinema, where one is obliged to accept the equivocal role of being physically part of an audience, the more essential distances are decently maintained). Mad King Ludwig of Bavaria built a private playhouse so that he could watch Wagner's operas quite alone; today, every owner of a television set enjoys a similar privilege. Indeed, one's privilege is greater, for though the paranoid Ludwig could isolate himself from fellow spectators by refusing them admittance, he must have been uneasily aware that his lonely presence in the auditorium was perceptible – and potentially inhibiting – to the singers on the stage and the musicians in the orchestra pit.

If an actor works in an atmosphere of constant danger, it is also true that no member of an audience is ever entirely safe.

During *Re:Joyce!* a story is told of Grenfell on tour in Australia. Distracted by the persistent noise of sweets being unwrapped and consumed in the stalls, she stepped out of character and sternly informed her public that if they didn't sit still and keep quiet she wouldn't go on with the show. This is generally seen as a heroic gesture, in line with the legend of ladylike sanctity that has grown up around Grenfell's memory, but to me it sounds unattractively bossy, in the worst manner of Edwina Currie. To be forbidden to eat sweets in the theatre is surely an encroachment on civil liberties . . . I prefer the kind of theatrical anecdote which, though told as a joke, is offered as illustration of the deplorably unprofessional behaviour of some wayward *monstre sacré*.

Mrs Patrick Campbell, for example, hidden behind the screen in *The School for Scandal* while two elderly knights as Sir Peter Teazle and Joseph Surface crawled with maddening deliberation and pointless pauses through their scene. Suddenly losing patience, she boomed aloud for all to hear: 'Oh, *do* get a move on, you silly old pongers!' Or the one about John Barrymore as Richard III, after a heavy pub-crawl with his co-star Wilfrid Lawson, making such a hash of his opening soliloquy that a member of the audience called out, 'You're drunk!' – on which Barrymore approached the footlights and conspiratorially replied: 'Just *wait* till you see Buckingham!'

Re-read Chapter 47 of *Great Expectations*. Pip, like many a hero of more self-consciously paranoid novels, has a feeling that he is being followed but has so far failed to catch a glimpse of his pursuer. He visits a Thames-side theatre where his friend Mr Wopsle, an earnest but unsuccessful actor, is appearing in a mixed bill. Throughout the performance, Pip is uncomfortably aware that Mr Wopsle is looking straight at him – and sometimes, more puzzlingly, staring at a point just behind and to the side of where he is sitting. Afterwards, backstage, Mr Wopsle confirms this. He had been delighted to recognise Pip – less so to recognise the man who, for part of the time, had materialised 'like a ghost' in a nearby seat . . . This is how Pip learns for certain that Compeyson is on his trail.

The whole thing is narrated in Dickens's broadest comic vein (poor Mr Wopsle is ludicrously miscast in Grand Guignol and pantomime) and could be dismissed as a piece of obviously contrived plot-fabrication making shameless use of coincidence: yet its effect is deeply unsettling. The idea that Compeyson has been sitting so close to Pip without the latter being conscious of him is disturbing enough, but the fact that it is Mr Wopsle who has seen them both gives it an uncanny, aberrant dimension. For that isn't what is supposed to happen in a theatre – it's the wrong way round. Even with plays in which the audience is directly addressed from the stage, this audience is conceived as a composite, anonymous creature – and when actors, visited later in their dressing rooms, politely say, 'You were a wonderful audience,' it isn't the individual spectator who is being praised. By convention, each member of an audience is assumed to be either invisible from the stage or only vaguely discernible as part of an amorphous whole. But Mr Wopsle not only distinguishes Pip in the supposedly dark 'out front', he also notices something about him of which Pip is himself ignorant. The place of discreet concealment turns out to have been a scene of sinister discovery and exposure.

This complex, rather clumsy sequence of events could be

interpreted as intending to suggest that the stage, while apparently a window onto other lives, can also sometimes act as a mirror reflecting our own, or even as a penetrating x-ray photograph revealing a secret danger. But Dickens, of course, means nothing so pretentious. His genius shows more intriguingly in the way that, for all its strangeness, the episode is completely credible. Pip is agonisingly embarrassed by the spectacle of Mr Wopsle making a fool of himself, but it does not occur to him to leave the hall or even to turn round. If he had done so, he would have spotted Compeyson for himself. Some fiercer imperative than mere good manners prevents his escape and imposes at least the pretence of attention on him as a duty. One may fall asleep at the theatre, one may eat sweets noisily and offend Joyce Grenfell, one may even hiss and boo – but one cannot, it seems, look away.

1988

PART TWO
BOOKS

ELLE ET LUI

Colette: The Difficulty of Loving by Margaret Crosland
The Evening Star by Colette. Translated by David Le Vay
The Thousand and One Mornings by Colette. Translated by
Margaret Crosland and David Le Vay

M OST LITERARY CENTENARIES ARE ESSENTIALLY MEANING-
LESS, carrying as they do a lunatic implication that the
value of a writer's work may be measured by some temporal
metric system. They can also be unfortunately timed to coincide
with a reaction of public apathy after an overdose of immediately posthumous acclaim. To this, as to so much else, Colette
is an exception. Freed by age from the spurious element of
scandal, her best books seem even better today than when she
wrote them, while the worst have only dated in a charming
way, like an *art nouveau* vase or a music-hall song of the *belle
époque*. Also, one feels that she *should* have lived to be a hundred,
that the wise, white witch of the Palais Royal, most earthy of
oracles, should still be available as an object of pilgrimage.
Certainly, there would be no disappointing ambiguity about
her utterances which, like those of a really good fortune-teller,
would consist of constructive advice on affairs of the heart and
practical domestic problems: and yet a touch of magic would
not be entirely absent from the consultation.

These three companion volumes constitute, I'm afraid, a
rather feeble celebration of the anniversary. Margaret Crosland's perfunctory biography – possibly written in haste to meet
the centenary deadline – adds little of importance to the material
already available in *Earthly Paradise*, an artful selection of Colette's own autobiographical writings made by Robert Phelps

and published by Secker & Warburg in 1966. *The Evening Star*, a book of recollections written during the Second World War, was one of the sources drawn on by Mr Phelps: it is now translated in full for the first time. *The Thousand and One Mornings*, a collection of bright but ephemeral journalistic pieces, is of interest only to the most advanced and incurable Colette addict. Luckily, a major part of Colette's considerable *œuvre* is already available in English, much of it in paperback.

Even during her life, Colette enjoyed a literary reputation independent of textual analysis: Henri de Montherlant wrote that there was nothing to explain and nothing to criticise about *Chéri* – all you could say was 'That's it'. Since her death, her achievement has been interpreted as the wider reflection of a personal myth, and she is now canonised as a secular saint whose vision pierced the veil of a purely sensuous paradise on earth. The Archbishop of Paris was severely criticised when he refused her a Catholic burial, but surely he was paying her a compliment. Mysticism is conspicuously absent from her work, which celebrates the pleasures and pains of the flesh with a concentration that almost seems to confer holy status on natural phenomena; and while she never attacked religion, she can be said to have undermined metaphysical speculation by creating an equally exalted physical alternative.

Neither can she qualify as an ethical humanist: preserving her quick brain from the fatigues of unnecessary intellectual exercise, she consistently refrained from passing judgment on political and moral issues. Her life seems to have been one long, intent gaze – at animals, at plants, at human bodies. If her books are not exclusively 'visual', it is only because her other four senses were as sharply developed as that of sight. It is one of the greatest ironies in the history of literature that the kittenish daring of the Claudine books, more saucy than salacious, should have contained the seeds of a serious artistic exploration which eventually bordered on the solemn.

To sustain her in her mission, she thought it necessary to invent a sort of super-saint, and to find this earth-mother she looked no further than her own. Sido's wise, womanly letters have often struck me as being a bit too good to be true; and it now appears that some of these were doctored by Colette. The most famous, quoted in *La Naissance du Jour*, is from the dying Sido who refuses to visit her daughter for fear of missing the rare flowering of a pink cactus. Some daughters might have taken offence at this, even detecting between the loving lines a rather far-fetched excuse; but Colette writes that she is more proud to be the child of the woman who wrote that letter than of anything she may have achieved on her own. Recently, however, another letter has come to light, written by Sido at the same period, in which she quite simply accepts the invitation . . . It is possible that, while evoking her earthly paradise, Colette occasionally permitted herself a little of the licence granted to those writers whose preoccupation has been with the other world.

Somewhere between the naughtiness of her beginnings as Claudine and the dignity of her apotheosis as a pagan saint there is another Colette, whose memory will, I believe, outlive the others. This is the classical novelist, concerned with classical themes: love, jealousy, renunciation, despair. Within this category, *Chéri* and *La Chatte* seem to me indubitably masterpieces; some might add *Le Toutounier* or *La Seconde* to the list, others *La Vagabonde*, although I personally prefer its less famous sequel, *L'Entrave*. (It is incidentally curious that two of the most perfect of modern novels, *La Chatte* and J. R. Ackerley's *We Think the World of You*, should share the same theme: a love affair between a human and an animal. Not, one might have thought, the most promising *donnée* – but after reading them both one can only echo Montherlant's 'That's it'.) Several of her short stories – *Chambre d'Hôtel, Bella Vista, Le Képi* – might qualify as minor masterpieces. These usually start with Colette arriving at a hotel (she is as good on hotels as she is on courtesans and cats) where she becomes tentatively involved in a human drama. Reluctantly curious, she observes it unfold with an offhand accuracy before drifting back to her own concerns. These tales are unforgettable partly because the original narrative device is so successfully poised between the two clichés of camera-like objectivity and sensitive egocentricity.

I imagine that every great woman novelist, with the exception of George Eliot, has been told at one time or another that she 'couldn't draw a man'. The complacent, dismissive phrase is seldom strictly true. Few such writers attempt to draw a male character from his own point of view, but by presenting him from the outside in his relationship with women they often achieve a likeness uncomfortably close to the original. Margaret Crosland reiterates this criticism of her subject, making exceptions of Chéri, Alain in *La Chatte* and Phil in *Le Blé en Herbe*: 'It is as though she preferred to write about men who had not yet moved too far from the potentially bisexual state of childhood and adolescence.'

Colette herself assented to this view. In a passage from *The Evening Star* she apologises for the unreality of Renaud, the hero of the Claudine books, and continues:

> But the Maxime of *La Vagabonde*, the Jean of *L'Entrave*, were hardly any better . . . Not knowing how to deal with my own inadequacies I condemned them to idleness and allotted them as fields of action only the bed or the divan. Sensuality is no career for an honest man.

Here, I believe, Colette is being not only unfair to herself but also uncharacteristically conventional. She goes on to concede that Farou, in *La Seconde*, was 'less artificial' – but can she have forgotten the husband in *Chambre d'Hôtel*, a brilliant portrait of masculine weakness with whom it is possible to sympathise even through the medium of Colette's openly expressed dislike? And surely she must have realised that this 'inadequacy' was itself the explicit theme of *L'Entrave*? In that merciless novel, Renée Néré knows that she is older than Jean and assumes that she is more intelligent. Impelled by a conscious mixture of pride, humility and embarrassment, she insists on treating him as a beautiful sexual object who is also somehow second-rate as a human being. This insultingly patronising attitude is the pathetic weapon of a desperate woman determined to forestall another injury to her self-confidence. It turns out to be a fatal tactic. Imprisoned in an artificially physical relationship, Renée and Jean find that all other forms of communication have become impossible.

'What's the matter with you?'
'With me? Nothing.'

One of us would sometimes ask the question, sometimes make the reply: we had almost reached a point where our conversation consisted entirely of these few words.

It is Renée who invites our sympathy but the instinctive artist in Colette sees to it that Jean gets his share – and it is not the kind of sympathy accorded to a dummy. This book is also a valuable corrective to that quality in Colette which can sometimes faintly irritate – a touch of conceit. In spite of the agonies they go through, these experienced 'older women' do tend to be rather too pleased with themselves. I shall never forget the infinite condescension of Edwige Feuillère, playing Mme Dalleray in a film version of *Le Blé en Herbe*, when after seducing the sixteen-year-old hero she addresses him tenderly as *'petit mendiant'*. (However, the relevant passage in the book makes it clear that Mme Dalleray is the 'beggar' – one of the sort who 'drink in the illusion that they are the generous donors'.) A few wisps of her own era clung to Colette, who in the main was so far in advance of it – an era when sexual adventure was seen as a solemn rite where men were supplicants and woman 'gave themselves'. It is true that she reversed the sexual roles, but by casting her pretty heroes as virgins who put a high price on their bodies she subtly enhanced the self-esteem of her worldly-wise heroines who 'to beg were not ashamed'. In *L'Entrave*, this slightly bogus assumption of sexual superiority is analysed out of existence by her own uncompromising honesty.

Yet we learn from *The Evening Star* that she considered *L'Entrave* a failure. Begun while she was pregnant, it was interrupted by the birth of her daughter. In a revealing if somewhat affected passage, she writes:

My strain of virility saved me from the danger which threatens the writer, elevated to a happy and tender parent, of becoming a mediocre author, of preferring henceforward the advantages conferred by a visible and material growth: the worship of children, of plants, of breeding in its various forms. Beneath the still young woman that I was, an old boy of forty saw to the well-being of a possibly precious part of myself.

After reading that she considered sensuality no career for an honest man, it comes as a slight shock to learn that Colette designated the writing side of her personality as an 'old boy'. (If the original phrase was *'vieux garçon'* I suspect that 'old bachelor' may have been intended – but this interpretation by no means diminishes the shock.) It seems a betrayal of her triumphant bisexuality, her simultaneous recognition of profound differences between men and women and her heroic decision to ignore them. No one has equalled her ability to depict, unsentimentally and unsensationally, emotional relationships between women: lesbians in *Le Pur et L'Impur*, sisters in *Le Toutounier*, friends and rivals in *La Seconde*, mother and daughter in the various books consecrated to Sido. She can describe a milieu where men are excluded and convince one that they are not missed. It is therefore surprising to find that she saw writing as a masculine activity and communion with nature as typically feminine – surprising that she should have separated them at all.

For her main achievement was to find a new way of narrowing the gap between art and experience: instead of writing about her life, she lived her books. Somerset Maugham made a fool of himself when he wrote of Colette:

> Such is the ease of her expression that you cannot bring yourself to believe that she takes any trouble over it . . . I was exceedingly surprised to hear that she wrote everything over and over again.

Colette's style, on the contrary, is intensely literary – even on occasion precious – and clearly the result of dedicated labour; but the content approximates so closely to what she really thinks and feels that an illusion of simplicity is produced. It wasn't an 'old boy' who managed this difficult feat, it certainly wasn't a *'vieille fille'*, but the totality of Colette: Sido's daughter, Willy's victim, Missy de Belboeuf's *petite amie*, the second-rate music-hall *artiste*, the lover of animals, the unsuccessful cosmetician, the wise old woman of the Palais Royal. And surely a part of her inspiration came from Chéri – spoiled, desirable, but doomed to solitude; a part from Léa – practical, resilient, a connoisseur of the senses; and perhaps a part from Saha, mysterious cat, unconscious of her own perfection.

1973

Behind the Bath

Douchka by Colette Audry. Translated by Peter Green
Beloved Cats by John Smyth

AN IRRITATING SNOBBERY DICTATES THAT BOOKS ABOUT WILD beasts are more likely to have literary distinction than those about domestic animals – pets. In fact, the elephants, lions and otters that figure so regularly on the bestseller lists have all been partially tamed, otherwise how could anything be written about them at all? And the sentimentality that makes a fetish out of the preservation of wildlife also finds some deep, if vague, significance in these semi-tamed wild animals, which are really freaks – neither pet nor beast. Domestic animals are much more rewarding, both to know in life and to read about. The relative sophistication of the dog or cat simplifies, and thus strengthens, the easily misunderstood human-animal relationship: nostalgia for the primitive (always a suspect emotion) is no longer in question.

But what *is* in question? Some answers are broached in Colette Audry's book, which won a literary prize in France, where it was called *Derrière la Baignoire*. It was behind the bath that Mme Audry's beautiful Alsatian bitch would hide when she fancied herself in disgrace; and where – 'so wretchedly at odds with life, so alien to her own nature, so changed and broken and desperate' – she died. Mme Audry's relationship with Douchka was a searing experience, from which she could only hope to recover by writing this book. She was startled by the passion she eventually developed for the dog, and interested to discover that this devotion is something quite separate from other human emotions, neither a substitute for them nor a rival, and yet just as strong. When Geoffrey Grigson, reviewing Gavin Maxwell, writes in a scolding tone, 'really the beast we should get on terms with in our adult years is the human one', he is propagating the fashionable assumption that love for an animal (as distinct from woolly wonder at 'wildlife' in general) somehow implies a disregard for humanity, a fear of involvement. It may do so, in rare cases; in some, it may imply merely an extension of self-love; but in most it exists as a thing in itself, like the enjoyment of art or sport, harmless, intense and fulfilling.

But it must be admitted that books about animals often seem unduly egotistic. There isn't much that *can* be written about them (their restricted personalities, which contribute towards their attraction in life, make poor copy), and the writer is driven to pad out the pages with personal details, often of a trivial kind. Even Mme Audry cannot avoid this. 'I corrected the proofs of a book and polished up my Italian a little,' she will suddenly tell us, for no good reason, and she refers throughout to Jean-François, Michel, Jacqueline, Jacques without explaining them. For all its sophistication, her book has the obsessive chattiness peculiar to the pet-lover's corner. 'Some friends of ours, the D——s, suggested an alternative . . . As a special treat she would be taken round daily for a romp with Cartouche, a big boxer belonging to a neighbour of theirs called Peggy.' This fleeting reference to Peggy recalls a passage in *Beloved Cats* by Brigadier the Rt Hon. Sir John Smyth Bt, VC, MC, MP:

> On Christmas Day, we always drive down to my brother Bill's house near Farnham for lunch. Peggy, his wife, is a wonderful cook and always produces the most succulent meals . . . Bill and Peggy have an ebullient corgi, Sandy, who looks upon cats as his natural enemies.

In most animal books, these fascinatingly pointless glimpses into the writers' lives provide the necessary light relief from the harrowing sagas of painful partings, runnings away, difficult housetraining, spaying and castrating, mating and littering, hard-pad, and worst of all the continual danger of small betrayals, which the human dreads and the animal seems to anticipate. In Mme Audry's case, the light relief assumes an almost desperate quality, at any rate in English. She presumably writes that aggressively colloquial prose often favoured by intellectual French women (Colette, most egotistic of all animal-lovers, did too) and in Peter Green's translation the deliberate jauntiness degenerates into a tipsy heartiness: 'Jean-François would fetch her a clout on the muzzle . . . down the road for a quick pee . . . I just gave her a good telling-off . . . flaunting her arsehole to the world.'

Mme Audry may lack the innocence of Sir John Smyth, but like him she understands that nothing short of total enslavement to an animal justifies the relationship. *Beloved Cats*, like most pet books, is written in the special, simplified language of addicted literature. Mme Audry's aim is to analyse the complicated process by which she arrived (almost unwillingly) at the addict's position: and to articulate those feelings of guilt, ecstasy and (after Douchka's death) despair which are usually conveyed in a conventionally stylised form. Very few serious writers have attempted this – at least, where domestic animals are concerned – and fewer still have succeeded: J. R. Ackerley has got nearer than anyone else to the heart of the mystery. It is Mme Audry's self-consciousness, her implied surprise that she of all people should be writing an animal book, which impedes her insight; also, she fusses too much about whether her own view of Douchka corresponds to the 'real' Douchka. In her agony of remorse after the dog's death, for which she blames herself, she sometimes descends into bathos. 'She never deliberately lied to me. How could she lie? She had no language.' But the insight is there: somewhere between the slangy, 'sensible' start and the haunted misery of the close. For the truth is simple. She faces it in a sentence: 'Between two human beings there is no such thing as "pure love", *in vacuo*; but the whole aim and purpose of owning a dog is to love it and be loved by it.'

1963

THE LAST YEARS OF THE MASTER

Henry James: Vol. V. The Master: 1901–1916 by Leon Edel

LEON EDEL HAS DEVOTED TWENTY-ONE YEARS TO WRITING HIS massive biography of Henry James, and in the introduction to this fifth and final volume he defends the length of the finished work. The implied note of apology is unnecessary: it is easy to believe his claim that the most drastic selection went into its preparation. How could so sensitive a scholar, engaged on this particular subject, ignore the exigencies of form and design? One could even perversely wish that he had been less selective, less concerned to shape the available material into a work of art of which the Master himself would have approved. If this book deserves a place among the very best literary biographies, it is through the diligent accumulation of detail, which steadily increases in interest as it mounts in volume. The recurrent themes with which he attempts to impose a pattern on this wealth of anecdote are less convincing. Some readers may feel, for instance, that just a little too much significance has been given to the novelist's association with Constance Fenimore Woolson, although the existence of their relationship is undoubtedly one of Mr Edel's most spectacular *trouvailles*. Compared with other recent exponents of literary biography, however, Mr Edel is commendably balanced: when establishing links between the life and the fiction of his subject, he is seldom more than tentative. Very rarely, his judgment wavers, as in his comments on James's insistence that his collected works should consist of twenty-three volumes. 'We might speculate about the significance of the combination of "two" and "three"

– and we might recognise that James had always been the "third person" in his relations with his mother and his brother; and then his Aunt Kate was the third person in a combination with his parents. Triangular relations are at the heart of his novels.' But then, possibly remembering that 'the eternal triangle' is at the heart of many other novels as well, Mr Edel comes to his senses, and makes the much more enlightening point that the collected works of Balzac – which had enormously influenced James – were available in twenty-three volumes when he first read them.

Mr Edel is also admirably cautious about the numerous apocryphal anecdotes, disseminated by Ford Madox Ford and others, with which the James legend later became encrusted. He probably never said or did many of the 'characteristic' things attributed to him: what he did, demonstrably, say and do and write are more than enough for his biographer and for us. Through these, he is revealed in all his formidable complexity: immensely kind but ruthlessly selfish; fastidious to the point of eccentricity but stoically tough-minded; socially conventional and sexually timid but intellectually a fierce champion of individual fulfilment. Such contradictions are to be expected in an artist who dedicated his life's work to the discovery and development, in widely differing situations, of the element of ambiguity.

Mr Edel's respect for the mystery of James's personality is matched by the judgment he shows in delineating the 'minor characters'. He is particularly good on Edith Wharton – about whom James wrote: 'She uses everything and everyone either by the extremity of strain or the extremity of neglect – by having too much to do with them or by being able to do nothing whatever – and passes on to scenes that blanch at her approach.' There is high comedy in the relationship between James and this snobbish, brilliant, insensitive, almost insultingly wealthy woman who hero-worshipped the writer but failed to appreciate his books. At one point, she tactlessly tried to raise a subscription fund for his benefit, imagining him much harder-up than he was; at another, she failed to charm his secretary, the intelligent and observant Theodora Bosanquet, by asking her to a conspiratorial tea and receiving her in an elaborate pink négligé and a boudoir cap of *écru* lace trimmed with fur. One of Mr Edel's most enjoyable pieces of detective work is the discovery, in James's story 'The Velvet Glove', of a concealed Max Beerbohm-like parody of Mrs Wharton's *The Fruit of the Tree*.

Luckily, James had other friendships, and the tone of each is subtly conveyed by his biographer. There was charming Miss Jessie Allen, high-spirited and tactful, whom he called 'Goody Two Shoes'; empty-headed, glamorous Jocelyn Persse; and, of course, the young Hugh Walpole, to whom James wrote: 'You bleat and jump like a white lambkin on the vast epistolary green which stretches before you co-extensive with life. I positively invite and applaud your gambols.' According to Stephen Spender and Somerset Maugham, Walpole once offered his body to James, and was rejected with the anguished cry: 'I can't! I can't!' Could this reaction conceivably be accounted for by the lambkin's insufficient physical attractions rather than by James's prudish terror of the beauties of the flesh, as is generally supposed? James's assocations with the famous (Conrad, Wells, Stephen Crane) are less intriguing than his relations with his servants. These include the diminutive Burgess Noakes, who matures from a grubby 'boots' via the army into James's faithful valet; his stately housekeeper, Mrs Paddington; and an extraordinary married couple, the Smiths. These were kindly treated by James and served him well for sixteen years as a model butler and cook; but their employer had failed to notice that his 'treasures' were steadily degenerating into alcoholics. Their final departure, in the last stages of delirium tremens, is an unforgettable episode: it is the sort of thing that was always happening to the Goncourts.

The biography reaches a magnificent climax with Mr Edel's account of the Master's last days. He suffered a stroke in his Chelsea flat on the morning of 2 December 1915: Minnie Kidd, the housemaid who found him lying on his bedroom floor, heard him say: 'It's the beast in the jungle, and it's sprung.' From then until his death on 27 February 1916, his mind intermittently wandered. No finer *donnée* could be imagined for one of James's own tales than the adventures of this super-subtle consciousness – with its supremely developed powers of accurate expression, its scrupulous discrimination and resolute rationality – as it confronted the confused, illogical and incommunicable experience of near-madness. Throughout this ordeal, his bemused brain remained unmistakably that of Henry James. 'I have a curious sense,' he said to those around him, 'that I'm not the bewildering puzzle to all of you that you are to me.' In his delirium he lost all sense of place, speaking at one moment of 'the curious annexation of Chelsea to Cork'. He suspected a plot to conceal his actual whereabouts from him, and was troubled by the fear that people were mocking at his mania. He dictated two mysterious letters: one from Napoleon to a brother and sister-in-law, giving them instructions on the redecoration of the Tuileries and the Louvre; and another, phrased in the same imperious terms, to his own brother and sister-in-law (although William James had been dead for six years). 'It sounded,' Mr Edel writes, 'as if he had gone out into the world and had conquered, and was allowing William and Alice to share in the spoils.'

For someone whose reason has become deranged to identify himself with Napoleon is a comically common occurrence, the subject of many a music-hall joke. But in the case of Henry James it may have an added significance. One of the things that distressed him on his deathbed was the lack of male company: he complained, probably for the first time in his life, of being surrounded by women. A fashionable doctor, consulted by James during his last visit to New York, gave it as his opinion that the novelist had 'an enormous amalgam of the feminine in his make-up'. As James himself might have put it, *ça se voit*. Most of his intimate friends were women; in his romantic attachments to younger men, the maternal element seems to have been stronger than the erotic; his respect for conventional forms of behaviour (illustrated by his shocked repudiation of Violet Hunt) had a fussy, old-maidish quality; the things that interested him – and furnished the plots for his novels and stories – were of the kind that is supposed to interest women rather than men.

Yet, of other novelists, it was the vigorous art of Balzac that he most admired, and he saw his own work, and the values which he sought to make it reflect, as essentially masculine in character. He seems to have considered that the ability to face the truth must be a male prerogative. Basil Ransom, in *The Bostonians*, complains that 'it is a feminine, a nervous, hysterical, chattering, canting age, an age of hollow phrases and false delicacy and exaggerated solicitudes and coddled sensibilities. The masculine character, the ability to dare and endure, to know and yet not fear reality, to look the world in the face and take it for what it is – a very queer and partly very base mixture – that is what I want to preserve.' There is something of the Napoleonic conqueror in the enterprise with which James invented new forms of expression and in the courage with which he used them to 'look the world in the face'. Nonetheless, a more typically 'masculine' character would perhaps (like Tolstoy) have wished to do something more with the world than look it in the face. Both James's greatness and his limitations as an artist seem to me to be suggested by a letter he wrote to the sculptor Hendrik Andersen. James loved Andersen for his good looks and simple 'manly' nature, but deplored his lack of talent and clearly thought him rather a fool. 'The World,' he wrote, 'is a prodigious and portentous and immeasurable affair, and I can't for a moment pretend to sit in my little corner here and "sympathise" with proposals for dealing with it. It is so far vaster in its appalling complexity than you or me, or than anything we can pretend without the imputation of absurdity and insanity to do about it, that I content myself, and inevitably *must* (so far as I can do anything at all now), with living in the realities of things, with "cultivating my garden" (morally and intellectually speaking) and with referring my questions to a Conscience (my own poor little personal) less inconceivable than that of the globe.'

Civilised, ironic, eminently sensible – the note is typical of James. It is also a little smug. Better-known quotations strike a more exalted note. 'Art *makes* life, makes interest, makes importance'; 'Be generous and delicate and pursue the prize.' Art, for James, was a realm in which madness (in the form of fanaticism) had its place: life should be kept an orderly and temperate affair. The drama (of which there is plenty) in this biography is confined to the writing of his books, while his social existence is properly interpreted in terms of delicate comedy. As he lay dying, James the writer acquired complete control of James the social animal. He had already written his own epitaph: 'The rest is the madness of art.'

1972

BALZAC

Balzac by V. S. Pritchett

BALZAC, OBSESSED AS HE WAS BOTH BY PRINTING AND BY furniture, would have been fascinated by the concept of the coffee-table book. He loved luxurious objects, so long as he could convince himself that they were good buys, and this illustrated biography has the enduring solidity of a substantial *bibelot* in addition to its considerable literary merits. More than any other great novelist, Balzac was susceptible to glamour – a point missed by the many critics who have accused him of vulgarity. It might almost be said that he invented glamour, in its modern sense, although he can never have used the word, for which it is difficult to find a precise French equivalent. (My dictionary gives *enchantement, charme, fascination, prestige, éclat,* all Balzacian nouns but lacking the suggestion of vulgarity inherent in the English, and even more so in the American.) The sumptuous illustrations which accompany, complement and enhance Pritchett's artfully condensed narrative seem to have been chosen in order to please its subject: they do more than decorate, they furnish his life. At the same time, they cast a glamour over it – as everyone knows, pictures of the past acquire an automatic and faintly deceptive charm. *La Comédie Humaine* was born when Balzac, graduating from the influence of Sir Walter Scott, decided that the present could be interpreted in the romantic terms hitherto reserved for the past. Writing the history of his own times, he saw them *as* history – saw them, possibly, in much the same way as we see them now. It is significant that he should have been the model for one of the first daguerreotype portraits. What an enthusiastic amateur photographer he would have been if he had lived a little later!

The lavish picture-book would be a meaningless medium in which to celebrate a more exclusively cerebral writer, but (as Angus Wilson has already proved with his similar book on a similar genius, Dickens) it can be a fitting tribute to a man who lived on the same prodigal scale as he wrote.

There is no reason to regret that Mr Pritchett (who has written elsewhere, and with great perception, about Balzac's work) should have chosen to concentrate here on his life. Instead of Pritchett the critic on Balzac the novelist, we are given Pritchett the novelist on Balzac the man. André Billy and André Maurois have dedicated exhaustive biographies to Balzac which, in spite of their various distinctions, have remained as difficult to finish as some of Balzac's own books where the original excitement is gradually dissipated by a mass of indigestible detail. Mr Pritchett approaches his subject in a delightfully dashing and arbitrary manner, concentrating on what has stimulated his own imagination, so that the result resembles one of those shorter novels in which Balzac was often at his best. Like them, it has as its central figure an eccentric personality of almost incredible proportions. There are episodes in this story which, if it had been presented as fiction, one might be tempted to disbelieve. 'I don't care for Balzac myself,' said Madame de Guermantes, 'I think he exaggerates.' Proust – Balzac's most spectacular heir – exposed the shallowness of this reaction:

> In general, she disliked people who 'exaggerated', and were thus an implied rebuke to those who, like herself, did not; people who gave 'exaggerated' tips, which made hers look exceedingly stingy, people who felt a more than ordinary degree of sorrow at the death of a relation, people who did more than is usually done for a friend in distress, or went to an exhibition expressly to see any picture that was not a portrait of someone they knew or 'the thing to see'.

Thus the society lady reveals her own pusillanimity and philistinism in a ready-made phrase which might pass as fastidious in the *faubourg*. Proust, Dickens and Balzac all understood in their different ways that some aspects of real life are so extraordinary that to exaggerate them is an impossiblity. They refused to allow a 'sense of proportion' to vitiate that sense of wonder which gives the initial stimulus to artistic expression.

Take, for example, Balzac's love affairs, which consumed a great deal of his time and energy but were considerably less important in his life than his hideously complicated financial interests and the creation of his fictional world. His first love was Madame de Berny, twenty-two years older than Balzac and the mother of nine children, a respectable provincial matron who remembered the court of Louis XVI. After a slow seduction, he awoke in her a sexual passion which lasted till her death. She lived to read his portrait of her in *Le Lys dans la Vallée*, which she criticised because it presented their relationship as platonic. Of her he wrote:

> Mme de Berny, although married, was like God to me. She was mother, mistress, family, friend and admirer; she made me a writer and consoled me as a young man, she formed my taste, she wept and laughed like a sister, she came to me every day to soothe away my pains like a sleep . . . More, although she was under the thumb of her husband, she found a way of lending me 45,000 francs and I paid off the last 6,000 (with 5 per cent interest of course) in 1836. But she rarely raised the question of the debt . . .

How quickly Balzac can pass from the sublime to the sordid, from God to 5 per cent interest!

Poor Madame de Berny lost him, not to a young girl, but to another middle-aged woman – the Duchesse d'Abrantès, a member of the parvenu Napoleonic nobility who had been the mistress of Metternich. Mr Pritchett describes her as

> a small stout woman, carelessly dressed in coffee- and even opium-stained clothes and shabby shoes; but the uncorseted aristocratic slattern with dark hair all over the place was famous for her toilette and she wore the fashionable shawl like an empress. Her voice was hard, mocking and precise. Her nose was a large and aggressive beak. She was said to be a good-natured liar but very charming with it. She was soaked in perfume. A scurrilous Versailles lawyer called Lambinet said that this was because she smelled like a polecat. But Balzac's imagination was carried away by her history and her distinction.

Even higher in the social scale was Madame de Castries, who had been crippled in a hunting accident and walked with a stick:

> What impressed him was that she was the wife of a marquis who later became a duke, a real Legitimist from whom she had long been separated. Soon after her marriage she had loved the son of Metternich and had a son by him . . . Then, tragically, her lover had died.

The Marquise allowed Balzac to hope that she would become his mistress, but at the crucial moment refused to do so, giving as her reason that her lover's death and her accident had been God's punishment for adultery. He had an easier success with the Contessa Guidaboni-Visconti, born Fanny Lovell of Cole Park in Wiltshire, a jolly English girl who was promiscuous in a high-spirited way and may have borne him a son. Finally, there was Madame Hanska – the fat, intense, humourless, possessive Polish aristocrat who dazzled him by her wealth, maddened him by her jealousy, and finally married him just before his death which her despotic and indecisive behaviour had probably hastened. Reading about these marvellous, ridiculous women, one feels that they must have been invented by Balzac himself. Each character has that peculiar individuality which can survive a romantic treatment, like grotesque crags seen through a beautiful mist. To revenge himself on the heartless Madame de Castries, Balzac spitefully put her into *La Duchesse de Langeais*. The tactic misfired: all he did was create a heroine larger than life. On his deathbed, he said to a friend: 'Send for Bianchon' – the doctor he had created in *La Comédie Humaine*. Mr Pritchett tells us that these most haunting of all last words have been disputed. Whether Balzac uttered them or not, he must have known that in the face of mortality imagination was the only cure.

1973

Updike

Rabbit Redux by John Updike

JOHN UPDIKE IS A SUPREME STYLIST WHOSE PROSE IS BOTH resonant and precise: but the effort to achieve these qualities has clearly been a strain. Carefully packed with poetic allusions, verbal fancies, evocative vernacular and calculated shocks, his paragraphs are presented to the reader like a series of bulging suitcases: when opened, their contents are revealed in an uncrumpled condition, good as new, but unavoidably flattened. The neatness, the compression, give them an unnatural look – unnatural, rather than unreal. He is a clever and beautiful writer who is obsessed by stupid people and ugly places, with the result that his books make a curious effect of perversity. In these sophisticated literary cocktails, the exquisite and the vulgar are fastidiously combined to produce a subtle transposition of aesthetic sensibilities: the chemical aftertaste of the vanilla shake on sale at the Burger Bliss is appreciated as though by the palate of Des Esseintes. Few other writers have taken such delicate pains to convey in words the untranslatable sensations of sexual experience. With the detached connoisseurship of an erotic *Michelin Guide*, Updike endlessly diversifies and tabulates, discriminating not only between different ways of making love but within each variety itself. When two of his characters are allowed to bring off a three-star suck, for example, we are invited neither to envy their success nor to share in their pleasure: we merely register the grade.

To a descriptive writer as insistently aware as Updike of the obvious fact that human beings live largely through their senses, sight, sound, smell, taste and touch present as great a challenge as sex. It is a challenge which Updike meets with a desperate determination, in the same dogged way that heroes of American novels are bent on proving their potency. Hence the sense of strain. The writer's tool – his vocabulary – is doomed to ultimate inadequacy in the unequal contest with sensual reality, and to polish this tool too long and too deliberately becomes a form of self-abuse: the more expert the refinements that are brought to this lonely activity, the greater will be the sterility of the inevitable anti-climax.

In other words, it seems to me that Updike's scrupulous concentration on the physical existence of his characters paradoxically places them at a distance from his readers, who observe them with remote curiosity as if they were zoological specimens preserved in a thick glass tank. They gain from this a kind of clinical glamour, which gave *Couples* its powerful if unpleasant distinction as a valid metaphor for the Kennedy era, when middle-class America, unable to face the implications of its country's politics, turned inwards to build an alternative culture based on the exploration of sexual expression. The world of politics seemed far away from the erotic intrigues so gracefully and lovingly recorded in that novel, but its absence was marked enough almost to constitute a ghostly presence. In *Rabbit Redux*, substantial fugitives from that world are permitted to encroach on one of the sleeping, sleazy Pennsylvanian suburbs which are Updike's special geographical territory and which also define the limits of his spiritual landscape.

Harry Angstrom was last met ten years ago, in *Rabbit Run*, when he made a heroic attempt to break the pattern of passivity which had rooted him in the fly-blown town of Brewer with an alcoholic wife, and *did* run. It will be remembered that he soon came back, after his wife Janice had accidentally allowed their baby daughter to drown.

In this sequel, Rabbit is thirty-six: we find that the former athlete has run to nothing more than fat. The failure of his historic flight has left him more passive than ever, although he enjoys outraging liberal convention by supporting the war in Vietnam. 'It's not all war I love,' he protests, 'it's *this* war. Because nobody else does.' Contentedly discontented, he has a dull job as a typesetter; what he erroneously assumes to be a mutually satisfactory sex-life with Janice; and a thirteen-year-old son, Nelson, whom he keeps on mistaking for a girl because of his long hair. It is 1969, the year of the Moon landing, and Kubrick's film 2001 is playing at the local cinema. This time, it is Janice who runs – no great distance, but far enough to share Homeric sexual delights with her Greek lover.

Rabbit's passivity is further intensified by this development. He allows a girl of eighteen, Jill, into his house: she's a rich dropout, sickened by the System. Jill is soon followed by Skeeter, a young Negro in hiding from the police, who has transcended the more orthodox ideas of the Black Power movement and believes himself to be Jesus Christ. Jill has an innocent friendship with Nelson; sleeps conjugally with Rabbit; blows Skeeter when he tells her to. Skeeter gets Jill hooked on hard drugs; Rabbit, passively smoking pot, does not react when his scandalised WASP neighbours lodge menacing complaints. He is making love with an old friend, Peggy Fosnacht, when the neighbours set fire to his house and Jill is burned to death. The police suspect Skeeter, and Rabbit helps him escape. Then Rabbit is declared redundant and, jobless, moves into his parents' home, where his mother is dying of Parkinson's disease. Janice comes back to him. Their reconciliation takes place in a sad motel bedroom, and the last words of the book are typical of the whole in the hermetic preciosity with which they describe a tentative conjugal encounter: 'He slides down an inch in the cool sheet and fits his microcosmic self limp into the curved crevice between the polleny offered nestling orbs of her ass; he would stiffen but his hand having let her breast go comes upon the familiar dip of her waist, ribs to hip bone, where no bones are, soft as flight, fat's inward curve, slack, his babies from her belly. He finds this inward curve and slips along it, sleeps. He. She. Sleeps. OK?'

Well, I'm not sure that it *is* OK. All this fine writing about curved crevices and polleny orbs has only succeeded in obscuring the author's more conventional but equally remarkable gifts for narrative, dialogue and psychological characterisation. One gets tired of being reminded that Jill's satiny ass resembles an upside-down Valentine – and yet, in between such similes, Updike has succeeded in making her come alive as a person. I still can't visualise her ass as clearly as I should like, but I do feel that I know what she thought about life and her place in it. Therefore, when I read about her death, I was distressed – and particularly distressed for Nelson, who (in spite of having reached puberty) is allowed by his creator to respond to the nightmare around him with intelligence, affection and straight-forward dismay. But Jill's death, and its effect on Nelson, are presented as incidental to the main theme of the novel, which is Rabbit's passivity. After the tragedy, he admits to his sister: 'I learned some things.' 'Anything worth knowing?' she asks, and he replies: 'I learned I'd rather fuck than be blown.' 'Sounds healthy,' is her comment. 'Rather unAmerican, though.' He tries another answer: 'I learned the country isn't perfect.'

But here he is interrupted by the author, who writes: 'Even as he says this he realises he doesn't believe it, any more than he believes at heart that he will die. He is tired of explaining himself.' At this point, an unworthy thought entered my mind: is Rabbit tired of explaining himself only because Updike is suddenly tired of explaining him? And is Updike tired of explaining him because there's nothing to explain? Beyond, of course, the *aperçu* that a two-star fuck is better – perhaps because less passive – but, anyway, *better*, than even a three-star suck?

1972

124

Sliced Life

Birds of America by Mary McCarthy

A TWENTIETH-CENTURY VERSION OF FLAUBERT'S DICTIONARY of *idées reçues* would surely include a list of the clichés spawned by the fashionable fear of pollution and its attendant cult of conservation. 'The quality of life', 'the population explosion', 'the problem of leisure', 'the Department of the Environment': such ready-made phrases have the complacent pomposity peculiar to an embattled bourgeoisie and one can imagine them on the lips of Monsieur Homais or one of Dickens's windbags. Separated by repetition from their unpalatable meanings, they have acquired the comforting properties of magic incantations: to utter them is to be absolved from action. Thus we have the modern paradox of the tourist brazenly complaining of the presence of tourists, apparently unaware that in discovering some Greek island to be 'still unspoilt' he is inevitably spoiling it himself; and the dilemma of the cultured progressive who finds that the righteous accents of protest now bear an embarrassing resemblance to the peevish whine of romantic reaction.

I can think of few subjects more worthy of the attention of Mary McCarthy, whose sympathetic malice has often shown itself in the past to be particularly sensitive to the confusions and pretensions of liberal attitudes; and in some degree it provides the theme of her latest novel. The first two chapters are set in New England in the early sixties, where the hero's mother, a musician harmlessly in search of the (mainly culinary) values associated with her traditional American youth, fights a losing battle against processed food and detergent powders. Her gradual degeneration from stubborn sentimentality into an almost hysterical despair is scrupulously recorded: taste becomes hopelessly confused with ethics until, as her son observes, for Rosamund the difference between sliced and unsliced bread is identified with the difference between right and wrong. This episode gives Miss McCarthy scope for further exploring one of her favourite narrative techniques, the catalogue: as some actors are said to be able to extract drama from a reading of the telephone directory, so can she find unexpected comedy in a series of shopping lists.

The remaining eight chapters follow Rosamund's son Peter, who is nineteen years old and Italian–Jewish on his father's side, to Paris and Rome; and the book turns into an extended essay, lavishly illustrated by anecdotes, on what it is like to be an innocent American abroad in Europe today. Throughout a succession of mildly ironic encounters, Peter is called upon to react to the bombing of Hanoi, the logic of vegetarianism, individual responsibility for general social evils, the relation of art to politics, and other pitfalls in the path of adolescence. Independent, original, sensitive, with a highly developed moral sense but in no way a prig, Peter is almost 'too good to be true' (although in the novel these words are applied by him to his mother). His bewilderments become less and less funny and as they succeed each other the book steadily diminishes in intensity. Miss McCarthy seems to have gone rather soft on her hero, although now and again she dutifully (but unconvincingly) introduces a note of scorn ('he had decided to be interested in art this year') as if he were a member of The Group. Her habit of standing a platitude on its head can be counter-productive: sometimes, even upside down, it remains a platitude. Similarly, she often introduces a character in order to make the point that he or she is a stereotype: in life one can be 'amusing' about people by likening them to stock figures in popular literature, but in fiction the implication falls flat.

I believe that the main reason for the dilution of the novel's impact is that the author has herself been infected by Rosamund's hysteria: she came to mock, as it were, but remained to applaud the muddled fight to restore civilisation's vanishing standards. Peter, a nature-lover, is savaged by a black swan in the Jardin des Plantes and ends up in the American Hospital.

Here he has a delirious vision in which he is visited by his idol, Immanuel Kant, who breaks the news to him that 'Nature is dead.' It is as if Miss McCarthy had invented her modern Candide in order to make the brutal point that Voltaire's famous escape clause has been annulled by technological growth: to cultivate one's garden – an activity no doubt involving the use of chemical fertiliser – is merely to do one's bit towards polluting the world.

Birds of America, then, is a *roman à thèse*. The thesis may itself be familiar, but the author has succeeded in constructing some ingenious variations on its basic message of despair. While acknowledging its importance, she simultaneously recognises a triviality in the human response to its challenge. This characteristic contradiction in her approach to her theme has, in earlier books, resulted in a tough brilliance, a loss of sympathy but a gain in clarity: in this case the conflict between precision of intellect and depth of feeling has unexpectedly produced an overall slackening of tension, as though a balancing act were being performed on a rope slung a few feet from the ground.

1971

EVA TROUT

Eva Trout by Elizabeth Bowen

THERE IS ONE THEME (OR RATHER, ONE SITUATION) THAT HAS often recurred in Elizabeth's Bowen's work: the disruption of a group of people caused by the inconvenient presence among them of a young woman or girl with an approach to life that is subtly different from theirs. These heroines have a disturbing effect owing to some imbalance in their sensibilities. They can be seen as either admirably well endowed with emotional integrity, or as fatally lacking in worldly sense: Miss Bowen's own attitude remains ambiguous. Thus, *The Death of the Heart* can be read as a tragedy of innocence betrayed by corruption, or as a social comedy about a tiresomely intense adolescent. Emmeline, the reserved, myopic heroine of *To the North*, blunders perversely into a love affair and precipitates a crisis with which she cannot cope; Jane, in *A World of Love*, falls in love with the *idea* of falling in love and her trance-like state upsets everyone in her orbit. Other examples can be found in short stories: the governess who has been tried for murder in 'Reduced', the little girl involved in some unmentionable (and therefore unmentioned) scandal in 'The Easter Egg Party', by their passive presence cause a displacement in the psychic atmosphere. Miss Bowen is usually assumed (probably with justification) to be on the side of the vulnerably sensitive; but part of her subtlety is to show how the victim, in her martyrdom, claims victims of her own.

Eva Trout is an extreme variation on this theme. Extreme in two senses: the situation itself is more obvious here than before, but its interpretation is more obscure. Large, handsome, an orphan and a millionairess, Eva has all her faculties but is at the same time mysteriously deprived. She cannot quite slot into life – an unsatisfactory upbringing provides only partial explanation for her unwieldy, recalcitrant and alienated personality. To see her as an eccentric is to over-simplify; she is nothing so ordinary as that. Neither is she straightforwardly immature in the sense of arrested development. She lives her life as a charade – it is not so much a question of fantasy as of pretence. She announces that she is going to have a child – then literally buys one, just as children are told they were 'bought at Harrods'. She assumes her maternal role with dedicated responsibility, but remains like a child playing with a doll; and the baby grows up to be deaf and dumb. When, eight years later, she falls in love with a boy much younger than herself, she proposes a make-believe marriage – a mock wedding in which she can 'play brides' without legal ceremony or sexual consummation. As soon as a genuine relationship becomes a possibility, the artifice she had created proves stronger than reality and she is destroyed.

Perhaps *Eva Trout* should be read as an ironic analysis of the romantic temperament – *Northanger Abbey* with a tragic ending, a sinister version of *Sense and Sensibility*. Certainly Miss Bowen's great distinction and originality as a writer of imaginative fiction have depended on the subtle fusion of two separate gifts: for social comedy, and for sensuous poetic intensity. Better than any other contemporary novelist, she can load a physical experience, however momentary, with profound emotional significance; at the same time, her view of her characters (when they are not thus isolated in subjective transports) can be critical, objective and exact. From her first novel, *The Hotel* (1927), to her seventh, *The Heat of the Day* (1949), these gifts were triumphantly combined: in my opinion the combination produced four masterpieces in *The Last September*, *Friends and Relations*, *The House in Paris* and *The Death of the Heart*. (I do not subscribe to the theory that Miss Bowen's best work is found in her short stories, brilliant as these often are.) With *A World of Love*, she leant rather heavily on the poetic side of her talent, to the detriment of the other; and the novel which followed this, *The Little Girls*, was presented as a comedy. The plots of *The Little Girls* and *Eva Trout* have an element of eccentric fantasy absent from her earlier novels (though present, I suppose, in the ghost stories), and the intentions of both books are less immediately plain. (That is to say, they resemble riddles to which there may not be a totally satisfactory answer: the answer no longer seems to be the simple fact of the book's existence.) Meanwhile her expressive and individual literary style, which had become noticeably mannered in *A World of Love*, has further developed in this direction with the two later novels. Do the verbal mannerisms help the writer to propound her riddle in its intricate entirety, or are they assumed to prevent the reader from solving it?

The blurb for *The Little Girls* suggested that 'it should be read with that attention to detail generally accorded to a detective story' as it contained little explanation but many clues. I think I may have found two clues in *Eva Trout*. Mrs Arble, a clever young woman with a literary mind, visits the Dickens house in Broadstairs (an apparently digressive episode in the story's structure). 'What,' she wonders, '*had* Henry James, that Dickens really had not? Or if he had, what did it amount to?' It would seem that Miss Bowen's own art was nearer to the social subtleties, the moral ambiguities and elegant reserve of James's world than the cruder, wilder, panoramic landscape over which Dickens energetically ranged. Yet her greatest achievement has been the communication of *feeling*: and few novelists have conveyed the essence of passion, terror and delight with greater power than Dickens. Is she perhaps experimenting, in her own way, with Gothic extravagance as a possible path towards the purity of emotion which formal classicism can only achieve in its greatest manifestations? A respect for the irrational seems to be coming nearer to the surface in her response to the sensual world.

At another point, Mrs Arble reflects: 'Imagining oneself to be remembering, more often than not one is imagining: Proust says so. (Or is it, imagining oneself to be imagining, one is remembering?)' Elsewhere, we are told that 'Time, inside Eva's mind, lay about like various pieces of a fragmented picture. She remembered, that is to say, disjectedly.' In other words, as in a dream. Proust and Dickens, so similar in their treatment of grotesque comedy, had a deeper affinity: Proust's obsession with memory was linked to the phenomenon of dreaming, and many passages in Dickens read like the uncanny articulation of a communal dream. Eva's mysterious deprivation resembles the disadvantage at which dreamers often feel themselves to be: the world around her is familiar, yet vaguely displaced; performance does not follow exactly on intention; memory is vivid but disjointed; she is unable to communicate with those around her, and yet they exist only because of her. It may be that *Eva Trout*, with its disturbing comedy and arbitrary development, can be best compared to *Alice in Wonderland* – if so, it is an *Alice* in which the satire is directed less at rational thought than at the treacherous logic of the emotional life.

1969

Come Along With Me

Come Along With Me by Shirley Jackson

S HIRLEY JACKSON BECAME BRIEFLY NOTORIOUS IN 1948, WHEN the *New Yorker* printed 'The Lottery' – a neatly harrowing short story with echoes of Hawthorne, which was included the following year in a collection of equally disturbing tales. Before her death four years ago, at the age of forty-six, she had also published six novels and two volumes of humorous domestic sketches. The latter achieved a middlebrow popularity; 'The Lottery' has remained an anthology piece; and one of the novels, *The Haunting of Hill House*, was made into an indifferent film. Comparatively few critics recognised the true nature of her unique and powerful talent; and her last book, which was posthumously published this year, has so far been more or less ignored by reviewers.

Come Along With Me is a rather bewildering assortment, edited by her husband, of an unfinished novel, fourteen stories which had not previously appeared in book form, and three disappointingly superficial lectures on the craft of fiction: but at least five of these stories are masterpieces in the peculiar genre which Shirley Jackson certainly perfected, and possibly even invented.

Her main subjects are madness, the supernatural and dreams: some combination of these elements can be found in most of her work. Her technique, however, is nearer to the delicate malice and sharp observation associated with the subtler forms of domestic comedy. If her literary father is Edgar Allan Poe, her mother is Jane Austen: no wonder that the artistic progeny of so unlikely a marriage has proved original enough to confuse categorisation.

The contents of *Come Along With Me* can be analysed in direct relation to her full-length books. The first four stories are prentice work, dating from 1938 to 1946, when the observant eye and accurate ear were being sharpened for later and more sinister use. 'Pajama Party', in which both cosiness and facetiousness are just avoided, belongs with the comic sketches of family life, *Raising Demons* and *Life Among the Savages*. The unfinished novel (which gives the collection its title) and 'Island' confront insanity head-on, recalling her explicit treatment of schizophrenia in the novel *The Bird's Nest*. 'A Visit', 'The Little House' and 'The Rock' evoke that obsession with houses which inspired two other novels, *The Haunting of Hill House* and *We Have Always Lived in the Castle*.

Shirley Jackson's treatment of the haunted house as a recurring subject differs from that of the traditional ghost-story writer. According to Freudian symbolism, to dream about a house is to dream about oneself; and confusion of identity is her central theme. This was, in my opinion, most successfully realised in an early and little-known novel called *Hangsaman*, published in 1951. A study of adolescent loneliness taking refuge in fantasy and almost slithering into madness, it is the more frightening for its light, unsolemn touch and occasional beady comedy. The seventeen-year-old heroine, whose first experience of college life acquires overtones of nightmare, is a blueprint for all victims of teenage breakdown: her painful self-absorption (are other people real?) is compounded by a growing uncertainty that that self exists (am *I* real?).

Something of the atmosphere of *Hangsaman* is recaptured by five stories in *Come Along With Me* – 'Louisa, Please Come Home', 'The Bus', 'The Beautiful Stranger', 'A Day in the Jungle' and 'The Summer People'. These all resemble waking dreams; or rather, they resemble those dreams in which one is able to convince oneself that, *this* time, one is not dreaming.

A girl runs away from home and lives a contentedly anonymous life in a nearby town, listening once a year to a broadcast appeal for her return. Finally, she does return: but her family sorrowfully reject her as yet another impostor seeking the offered reward. So she goes back to anonymity: 'My mother still talks to me on the radio, once a year, on the anniversary of the day I ran away . . . "Your mother and father love you and will never forget you. Louisa, please come home." '

An elderly lady falls asleep on a bus. The conductor wakes her and sets her down, bewildered, at a stop that is not her own: a deserted crossroads in the rain. With difficulty she gets a lift to a sort of roadhouse, which in spite of its squalor is disturbingly like the elegant house in which she was brought up. She is given a bed in a room exactly like her own, except that the wardrobe is in the wrong place. She sleeps, and has a nightmare – from which she is woken by the conductor to find herself back on the bus. He sets her down at a stop that is not her own: a deserted crossroads in the rain . . .

A middle-class matron meets her husband at the station on his return from a business trip. She knows at once that the man she meets is *not* her husband, but some stranger exactly like him who has been just sufficiently briefed to carry out the impersonation. After a few days, exactly like their previous life except for her unreasonable happiness, she goes into the town to buy him a present. Returning late, she stops the taxi at her house: then, when it has driven away, realises that the house is not hers. 'The evening was very dark, and she could see only the houses going in rows, with more rows beyond them and more rows beyond that, and somewhere a house which was hers, with the beautiful stranger inside, and she lost out here.'

In a rather similar story, a wife leaves her husband on an impulse, spends a happily aimless day in a hotel, and is then unaccountably overwhelmed by horror and fear. In yet another, an elderly couple who spend every summer in the country decide for once to delay their return to New York until after Labour Day: the break they have made with routine mysteriously provokes minor persecution from the villagers, and ultimately a hideous yet somehow reassuring terror.

Miss Jackson is most unsettling when she stops short of madness on the one hand, and the supernatural on the other, to concentrate on this glassy no-man's-land of the spirit which approximates to dreaming and yet has consequences in the waking life. Her characters suddenly lose their way and can never find it again because in the process they have forgotten their own names and addresses. The resulting sense of solitude is so cataclysmic that actual disaster is almost welcomed.

1969

ROMANTIC AGONIES

By Grand Central Station I Sat Down and Wept by Elizabeth Smart

ONE DOES NOT DEMAND PERFECTION FROM ROMANTIC ART. IT is a hit-or-miss affair, rather like gambling: the player hopes to win all but is resigned to winning nothing. And as the compulsive gambler is said to be basically more attracted by loss than by gain, so the romantic writer sometimes seems to court unnecessary disaster. Any attempt at the sublime must risk descent to the ridiculous, but there are moments in even the greatest romantic works (*The Sorrows of Young Werther, La Nouvelle Héloise, Wuthering Heights*) when the author seems to be making a deliberate approach to the absurd. The effect can be exhilarating: romantics are expected to make exhibitions of themselves. There is something almost holy about their folly.

The present novel was first published twenty-one years ago, under the auspices of Poetry London, and has remained a classic text of the romantic forties. A short book, it incidentally launched a fashion for long titles. Now it is reissued in paperback with an enthusiastic and ingenious foreword by Brigid Brophy, who writes that 'to the shame of those professing to practise criticism at the time, it made small stir' in 1945. I remember, however, that it *did* create a stir, at least in literary circles, although it never reached the wider public to which this edition will be available. Constructed as a single, sustained climax, it is like a cry of sexual ecstasy which, without changing volume or pitch, becomes a cry of agony. Metaphor breeds metaphor and allusions abound. The narrator is a young girl in love with a married man. That is the 'story': details of the salient episodes which, like Stations of the Cross, chart the progress of her passion are revealed only vaguely.

At one time, the romantic attitude to love involved renunciation, separation, and union in death. More recently, an adjustment has been made: 'To deny love, and deceive it meanly by pretending that what is unconsummated remains eternal, or that love sublimated reaches highest to heavenly love, is repulsive, as the hypocrite's face is repulsive when placed too near the truth.' If the old romanticism over-indulged a taste for the morbid, the new version has to guard against a priggish note. Young people, lacerated by experience, tend to become either morbid or priggish – that is, to deny the experience, or to enjoin it as a duty. Miss Smart was very young when she wrote this poem in prose, and (although neither priggish nor morbid) it is a young book which can best be appreciated by young readers. Youth – as distinct from immaturity – is an essential element in romantic art. She uses the vocabulary of youth – which delights in exaggeration and thrives on excess – with a rare discrimination. Not every pitfall, however, is avoided. In such books, the passages inspired by bitterness and betrayal tend to be more successful than those of lyrical fulfilment. 'Under the waterfall he surprised me bathing and gave me what I could no more refuse than the earth can refuse the rain.'

When the *donnée* belongs to the 'romantic novelist' school, the treatment, however literary, cannot always escape the banal. Such clever women as George Sand and Mme de Staël found the same. Brigid Brophy claims that Miss Smart *does* avoid bathos by incorporating mundane references, wittily using them to throw her apocalyptic vision into sharper relief. I would say that she is a true romantic who scorns to hedge her bets in this or any other way. Clearly capable of humour, she finds it, under these circumstances, beside the point. Humour presupposes a detachment which the subjective writer cannot afford.

This is a faceless book, peopled by sensibilities rather than characters. True to romantic tradition, the inanimate backgrounds are more vivid than the human beings who react to them: the poisoned Californian landscape ('Up the canyons the redwoods and the thick leaf-hands of the castor-tree forebode disaster by their beauty'), the innocent grandeur of the Canadian countryside ('Dear God, how sympathetic the frozen Chaudiere Falls seem under the December sky, compared with these inflexible faces'), the sordid hotel bedrooms in New York ('The wallpaper drips gloom, and the walls press in like dread'), play leading anthropomorphic roles in the interior drama.

Miss Brophy traces the novel's literary ancestry to Jewish liturgy (the Psalms and the *Song of Songs*) and classical legend (Ovid's *Metamorphoses*). She draws an illuminating parallel with Genet, but points out that Miss Smart's incantatory rhythms do not echo Catholic invocations to the saints. It is also true that this book is relatively free from the rather glib embellishment of Catholic guilt so pronounced in George Barker's *The Dead Seagull*, a similar treatment of an identical theme published some years later. The guilt so painfully evoked by Miss Smart is more humanist than religious. It is the lover's wife, not God, who has been offended, and the narrator's martyrdom is just as cruel as Christ's – 'Didn't the crucifixion only last three days?' But by the last page humanism has been rejected along with faith. 'I myself prefer Boulder Dam to Chartres Cathedral. I prefer dogs to children. I prefer corncobs to the genitals of the human male.' Embittered by the flesh, the romantic who once turned 'back to Nature' now cynically opts for artefact: the waters of Babylon flow under Grand Central Station. Here is the final metamorphosis – a re-interpretation of the anthropomorphic process itself. For if the classical spirit saw beasts, plants, mountains, rivers as imprisoned men and women, modern romanticism reverses the delusion: people become things, and the outraged sensibility defiantly merges into dripping wallpaper and Boulder Dam.

1966

IVAN BUNIN

The Gentleman from San Francisco and Other Stories by Ivan Bunin

IVAN BUNIN WAS BORN IN RUSSIA IN 1870, TEN YEARS AFTER Chekhov, whom he greatly admired and who became his friend. Chekhov often wrote to the younger man praising his work, although a letter in 1902 contains an interesting qualification: '"Pines" is very new, very fresh and very good, but too compact, like concentrated bouillon.' Bunin wrote two important essays on Chekhov, one on the occasion of the latter's death in 1904 and another a decade later. In the second article he made a significant point:

> For the past ten years they've been going on about 'Chekhov's tenderness and warmth' . . . All this makes intolerable reading. What would he have felt if he had read about his 'tenderness'? This is a word which one must use very rarely and very carefully about Chekhov.

Nonetheless, when Bunin's story 'The Gentleman from San Francisco' was translated into English by D. H. Lawrence and S. S. Koteliansky in 1922 and published in *The Dial*, Katherine Mansfield (who idolised Chekhov) wrote about it to Koteliansky in the following terms:

> There is something hard, inflexible, separate about him which he exults in . . . He just stops short of being a great writer because of it. Tenderness is a dangerous word to use, but I dare use it to you. He lacks tenderness – and *in spite of everything* tenderness there must be . . .

139

By this time, Bunin had become an exile. He left Russia at the time of the Revolution and lived in France until his death in 1953 – nearly half a century after Chekhov's. In 1933 he was awarded the Nobel Prize for Literature 'for the strict artistry with which he has carried on the classical Russian traditions in prose writing'. Even behind this tribute there lurks a qualification: the jury that year was fiercely divided between two separate first choices, and Bunin's victory was the result of a compromise. 'Too concentrated'; 'lacking in tenderness'; 'carrying on a classical tradition': such reservations have combined over the years to congeal into the received idea of a minor artist, perfect in his way but somehow deficient in creative power, restricted both in depth of emotion and breadth of imagination. The fact that most of the stories by which he became well known in Europe were written after 1917 and dealt with his memories of pre-Revolutionary Russia (as did also his novel, *The Well of Days*) has reinforced this sad impression of a vaguely irrelevant distinction founded on nostalgic charm. Yet, whether or not Bunin is a 'great writer', he is certainly a great original; anybody who has read a story by him is unlikely to forget it. This re-issue of fifteen of the best, chosen from three previously published collections long out of print, is therefore more than welcome.

Better even than Valery Larbaud (another neglected 'minor' writer), Bunin could evoke the transient but potent glamour of vast transatlantic liners and drowsy river steamers, of stuffily upholstered sleeping-cars and draughty station waiting rooms, of garish restaurants and hushed hotel bedrooms. These are often the backgrounds to the erotic encounters which he loved to describe, many of them brought to an abrupt end by the intrusion of violent death. They are in fact much more than backgrounds – for he created his own expressionist technique by which an almost oppressive wealth of sifted physical detail can succeed in interpreting the thoughts, feelings and actions of his characters through their immediate surroundings. Thus, although he was fascinated by the subject of sexual love, he never needed to be explicit about its performance: the highly charged decor did it for him. The results are among the most erotically exciting stories ever written.

The technique, however, can be used for other ends, as in

his most famous work, 'The Gentleman from San Francisco'. A self-made millionaire travels to Europe with his wife and daughter on the *Atlantis*. After dining at his hotel in Capri he has a fatal heart attack and makes the return journey in a coffin deep in the *Atlantis*'s hold. That is all there is to the story, and the central figure is scarcely characterised at all. Why is it a masterpiece? The meaningless opulence of the ocean crossing, the subtly sinister atmosphere of the voyager's arrival at Naples and Capri, are conveyed with such overwhelming force that psychological analysis becomes unnecessary; and Bunin's coup is to treat the undignified fate of the corpse as it is smuggled out of the hotel, off the island and back on to the luxury liner with an undiminished intensity, implying that the first-class passenger of the story's beginning was no more alive than the inanimate freight of its finish. No wonder Katherine Mansfield searched in vain for tenderness in this apocalyptic tale.

She might have found it in 'Sunstroke', another masterpiece on a smaller scale. Here a lieutenant and a young married woman pick each other up on a Volga steamer; surrendering to a sudden impulse, they leave the boat together at a small landing-stage and spend a night in a seedy hotel. She boards another steamer in the early morning, and he has to wait alone all day in this strange place for the next one. After she has gone, he realises that he is desperately in love with her – and that he does not even know her name. While he wanders restlessly around the little town, his obsession and frustration grow to unbearable proportions – and, as is usual with Bunin, the lieutenant's sufferings are defined by the almost hallucinatory vividness with which the place where he undergoes them is made real to the reader's senses.

In some of the stories, this insistent appeal to the senses can have an uncomfortable effect: one feels shut in with the scent of *Chypre*, the feel of dusty plush, the taste of 'juicy grouse cooked in well-fried sour cream', the sound of accordion music and the sight of lilac-coloured hoar-frost . . . Perhaps, to guard against surfeit, they should be read at carefully spaced intervals: the ideal reader would be perpetually unprepared for each elusive girl, each sweet adventure, each disruptive climax. These endings may at first sight appear to be arbitrary, but their seeds have been secretly present throughout – hinted at by the delicate morbidity with which Ivan Bunin celebrates the dangerous delights of his brilliantly tactile world.

1975

VALERY LARBAUD

(An Introduction to *Fermina Márquez*, translated by Hubert Gibbs, published by Quartet Books)

IT IS RARE FOR A WRITER TO BE BORN EXTREMELY RICH. IN many cases great wealth might prove a handicap to the development of a literary gift but Valery Larbaud (1881–1957) succeeded in turning his financial assets to artistically creative advantage. The source of his money was the Saint Yorre mineral spring at Vichy, which he inherited from his father at the age of eight: it could be said that, throughout the *belle époque* and the years between the wars, whenever a glass of Vichy water was drunk anywhere in the world a centime or so was added to Larbaud's fortune. The image thus evoked is wholly appropriate, for Larbaud was to become the poet of first-class travel, exploiting a sensibility perfectly attuned to the melancholy glamour of sleeping-cars, ocean liners and Ritz hotels.

> I felt all the sweetness of life for the first time in a compartment of the Nord express between Wirballen and Pskov. We were slipping through grasslands where shepherds, at the foot of clumps of big trees like hills, were dressed in dirty, raw sheepskins . . .
> Lend me your vast noise, your vast gentle speed, your nightly slipping through a lighted Europe, O luxury train! And the agonising music that sounds the length of your gilt corridors, while behind the japanned doors with heavy copper latches sleep the millionaires . . .

Throughout his childhood and adolescence Larbaud was dominated by his formidable widowed mother, whose control over his inheritance extended into his young manhood and under whose oppressive chaperonage he voyaged round Europe (but escaping her for long enough to enjoy discreet love affairs with young women in every country visited) while he wrote poetry, fiction and travel essays. His best-known work, *A. O. Barnabooth*, is a combination of all these genres, describing the spiritual, aesthetic and erotic adventures of a young South American millionaire as he fastidiously journeys along the same privileged, exotic routes that Larbaud had explored for himself. This was published in 1913; still not quite free of Madame Larbaud's influence, he was by then himself an influential figure on the French literary scene, a friend of André Gide and a prominent member of the group of intellectuals associated with the *Nouvelle Revue Française*.

Larbaud was a highly civilised example of everything that is understood by the phrase 'man of letters'. His sympathies, expressed in a vast output of literary criticism (including two collections with the overall title *Reading – That Unpunished Vice*), were generous and wide. An authority on Hispanic, English and American literature, he translated several Spanish and Portuguese writers into French as well as poems by Coleridge and Walt Whitman, prose by Sir Thomas Browne and Nathaniel Hawthorne, a novel by Arnold Bennett and almost the entire work of Samuel Butler. He also collaborated with James Joyce (and others) on the French version of *Ulysses*.

Larbaud had met Joyce in Paris in 1920 and had been excited by the parts of *Ulysses* that had so far appeared. The following year he published a long story called *Amants, Heureux Amants . . .* which was told as an interior monologue, and acknowledged its influence in the dedication: 'To James Joyce, my friend and the only begetter of the form I have adopted in this piece of writing.' Joyce immediately corrected him, pointing out that the true originator (and his own inspiration) was Edouard Dujardin, whose *Les Lauriers Sont Coupés* had been written as long ago as 1887: Larbaud, believing that he was introducing the stream-of-consciousness technique into French literature, was in fact merely reviving it. He made amends in 1923 by dedicating his next exercise in the genre, *Mon Plus Secret Conseil*, to Dujardin himself.

A passionate Anglophile, Larbaud paid several visits to

England and Wales between 1902 and 1914, vaguely researching a projected biography of Walter Savage Landor. His lyrical treatment of places which English readers may take rather prosaically for granted can sometimes be a cause of amused delight – in such poems, for example, as 'Madame Tussaud's', 'Matin de Novembre Près d'Abingdon' and 'Londres' (*'Les façades de Scott's, du Criterion, du London Pavilion/Sont éclairées comme par un soleil de l'Océan Indien'*) or in the story *Gwenny-Toute-Seule* which is set in Florence Villa, Stafford Road, Weston-super-Mare. In the charming novella *Beauté, Mon Beau Souci . . .* , which takes place for the most part in Chelsea, Queenie the heroine explains that she lives in *'Harlesden. Après Kensal Rise, dans cette direction.'* In her mouth, these names take on for the enamoured hero the melodious magic of enchanted groves . . . The humour here is intentional – Larbaud can be very funny. A group of poems attributed to his *alter ego*, Barnabooth the rich amateur, are subtitled *Les Borborygmes* – stomach rumbles, 'the only human voice that does not lie'.

In 1935, Valery Larbaud suffered a severe stroke which tragically incapacitated him for the remaining twenty-two years of his life.

Fermina Márquez, his first novel, was published in 1911, when he was thirty. It is set in Saint Augustine's, a boys' school just outside Paris – Roman Catholic and traditional but also cosmopolitan and rather dashing. Fermina herself is a young South American beauty who comes to visit her brother, a pupil at the school. The story examines the disturbing effect of her presence on some of the older boys – in particular on Joanny Léniot, the school swat, who identifies with Julius Caesar and makes a stern resolution to seduce her. But she is more successfully pursued by the handsome, sophisticated Santos Iturria from Monterey.

The model for Saint Augustine's was Sainte-Barbe-des-Champs, at Fontenay-aux-Roses, where Larbaud spent the happiest years of his childhood as a brilliant pupil from 1891 to 1894 – that is to say, between the ages of ten and thirteen. Here the seeds were nurtured of that *cosmopolitisme* which the adult Larbaud, in his life and work, was so fruitfully to epitomise. He put some of his own characteristics (his industry, his tim-

idity, his Roman self-discipline, his pride in scholastic achievement) into the figure of Léniot and others perhaps into that of
poor little Camille Moûtier, but Larbaud and his friends at the
college were in fact some years younger than the boys described
in the novel.

Larbaud in his later books was to write more smoothly than
he does in this one, which if judged by the highest standards
is not without flaws. The design is somewhat formless, and the
spontaneous ardours of post-pubertal emotion are occasionally expressed in a 'poetic' style which only narrowly avoids
embarrassing us. But as a psychological study of male adolescence it is on the whole delicate, touching and unsentimental,
while the faintly sinister atmosphere of this unusually glamorous school is evoked with a nostalgic vivacity that has proved
powerful enough to establish *Fermina Márquez* in France as a
minor classic. It seems to me one of those personal, intense,
romantic books which, if one responds to them at all, are likely
to haunt one with a peculiar poignancy for the rest of one's life.

1988

DREAMS AND DRAWING ROOMS

States of Grace: Eight Plays by Philip Barry. Edited and with a biographical essay by Brendan Gill

THE NATIVE SCHOOL OF DRAWING-ROOM COMEDY WHICH flourished on Broadway in the years between the wars never recovered from the death-blow delivered in the late 1940s by the first successes of Tennessee Williams and Arthur Miller. If George Kelly was the most original exponent of this vanished genre, Philip Barry was certainly the most distinguished, and *States of Grace* is a reminder of some of its more attractive qualities. Kelly's technique was to extract humour from the banalities of everyday dialogue, punctuated by obsessive and apparently aimless stage 'business', without attempting to enhance his material with the polish of wit. Barry, on the contrary, was bored by banality and conceived his characters as vehicles for wit; unlike many of his contemporaries, he did not pepper his plays with wisecracks but sought an elegant compromise between the current vernacular and the stylised speech of artificial comedy. This he only intermittently achieved, but the high points of his art generate a kind of earnest frivolity, a delicate and rather touching glitter, that are essentially American in inspiration and may be unique in the theatre.

The writers of American drawing-room comedy, at the same time fascinated by irresponsibility and appalled by vulgarity, found it difficult to celebrate the former without being guilty on occasion of the latter. In an effort to extricate themselves from this dilemma, they were sometimes driven (possibly by envy of Eugene O'Neill, a winner of the Nobel as distinct from the Pulitzer Prize) into an attitude of defiant apology. S. N. Behrman's *No Time for Comedy* is a characteristically defensive piece, about a successful commercial playwright called Gaylord Easterbrook and his wife Linda, a brilliant actress who stars in all his drawing-room comedies. A superficial socialite called Amanda Smith tries to seduce him by encouraging him to write a serious drama about 'death and the Spanish Loyalists'; and Linda has to exert all her subtle charm to keep him from simultaneously abandoning conjugal fidelity and the theatre of entertainment (the play vaguely implying a relationship between these hitherto separate concepts).

It seems that there was more than a touch of Gaylord Easterbrook about Philip Barry; sophistication was all very well, but a 'message' was somehow more classy. Unlike his friend Robert E. Sherwood, who profitably graduated from the arch trivialities of *Reunion in Vienna* to the shallow 'significance' of *Idiot's Delight*, Philip Barry never quite managed the transition. Although twenty-one of his plays were produced on Broadway, only a handful were hits: *Paris Bound* (not included in this collection), *Holiday*, *The Animal Kingdom* and *The Philadelphia Story*. All four were made into films (*Holiday* and *The Philadelphia Story* twice) and all four were drawing-room comedies. Just as Sherwood's success depended largely on the Lunts, and Behrman and Kelly wrote vehicles for Katharine Cornell and Ina Claire, so the plays by which Barry is remembered owed much to the actresses who appeared in them. Hope Williams created the roles of the wife in *Paris Bound* and Linda in *Holiday* on the stage; Ann Harding played these, as well as Daisy in *The Animal Kingdom*, on the screen; Katharine Hepburn played Linda in the remake of *Holiday*, starred in *Without Love* on both stage and screen, created Tracy Lord, the heroine of *The Philadelphia Story*, on Broadway, and immortalised her in the first film version. Williams and Harding are now forgotten, but Hepburn is still with us, and it is impossible to read the plays of Philip Barry without her peculiar intonations in one's inner ear. A line such as 'Oh, we're going to talk about me, are we? Goody' might go for little on the printed page if one had never heard what Katharine Hepburn made of it.

Barry was himself prouder of his serious flops than of his

tailor-made successes, but (to judge from the examples of both in this collection) the verdict of *Variety* and the Broadway public has been sadly justified by the passage of time. *White Wings* is a heavy-handed expressionist fantasy about the motor-car taking over from horse-drawn carriages; the Chekhovian *Hotel Universe*, with its cast of plangently discontented bright young things stranded on a terrace in the south of France, bears a closer resemblance to *Outward Bound* than to any more lofty model; and *Here Come the Clowns*, an allegory of Good and Evil played out by the freaks, homosexuals and similar misfits in a run-down vaudeville theatre, may have mystified the public in 1938 with its intimations of metaphysical despair, but today appears all too embarrassingly explicit. It seems that the frankly artificial framework of drawing-room comedy was necessary to preserve the frail but genuine spark of Barry's talent: when he ventured into freer forms, its originality was extinguished. Timid 'experiment' is doomed to date: masterly exploitation of a well-worn tradition may, with luck, transcend its context and achieve unexpected longevity.

In his informative but decidedly snobbish introduction to these eight plays by Philip Barry, Brendan Gill links their author with Eugene O'Neill, F. Scott Fitzgerald and John O'Hara, all of whom he sees as Irish-Catholic writer-outsiders 'intent upon acquiring the perquisites, both outward and inward, of their Protestant betters, with their country clubs and their cars and their chauffeurs and, above all, their assurance'. Speaking presumably as an Irish-Catholic writer-insider, Mr Gill seems to think that Barry made the adjustment more smoothly than the others:

> Resenting the WASP elect, O'Neill pretended to embrace its opposite . . . As for the rich in his plays, they are flimsy caricatures . . . he certainly never studied them at first hand, as, living among them, he might so easily have done . . . Fitzgerald had a sufficient entrée to the right houses and country clubs and, home on vacation, he would have been asked to the right winter dances and summer picnics . . . still, there were barriers that appeared insuperable, and the older he grew . . . the more bitterly he resented them . . . O'Hara was haunted by the mystery of Skull and Bones, the oldest and most distinguished of the secret societ-

ies at Yale . . . It was the most cherished of all O'Hara's day-dreams that if he had gone to Yale he would have been tapped for Bones. The touching truth of the matter is otherwise.

Barry, on the other hand, 'was partial to palaces and to the people who dwelt in them . . . Barry liked to be around lucky people and he set lofty standards of conduct for them. He wished them to be every bit as disciplined in their happiness as unlucky people are obliged to be in their misery. For both sorts of people the goals must be the same – grace of the body, grace of the spirit.' Mr Gill's concept of grace is in fact neither spiritual (as the title of the collection might suggest) nor even physical, but purely social: the appropriate adjective, one feels, would be 'gracious' rather than 'graceful'.

In his best plays about the rich (and his best plays *are* about the rich) Barry seems to be writing not as an outsider trying to crash the country club, but as an insider casting wistful glances at a happy-go-lucky artistic bohemia outside. Writers, painters and musicians – what Dorothy Parker ironically called 'people who do things' – are seen in such glamorous terms that one finds oneself forgetting the self-evident fact that Barry belonged in their company himself. *You and I* (1923), his first successful play, was originally called *The Thing He Wanted to Do* – and the thing that its hero, a middle-aged advertising executive, wanted to do was to paint. 'To look at him,' run the stage directions, 'you might think him any one of a number of things. You guess that he is in business and you know that he is successful. His hands – long, slender and restless – and a kind of boyish whimsicality in him, are all that betray the artist.' (There are moments when Barry himself betrays the influence of his near-namesake, the author of *Peter Pan*.) When Maitland White takes an overdue sabbatical from Madison Avenue in order to get down to his painting, his wife Nancy turns their loft into an impromptu studio. 'This room has been great fun for her,' the stage directions assure us, 'and she has been very successful in keeping out any suggestion of the "arty".' But has she? They continue:

At one side, there is a long refectory table . . . bearing two wrought-iron sconces, each containing six white candles . . . On the walls you will see Hokusai's *Fujiama* and *The Wave* – and very good prints they are. There are also two mounted heads of wild goats, upon the smaller of which a red Spanish beret is set at a rakish angle.

In Philip Barry's view of the leisured classes, 'taste' was at least as important an element as 'grace', and as one reads his plays one gradually begins to understand the criteria by which it is measured. 'Perfect taste' has nothing 'stuffy' about it – has even a touch of 'craziness'; but a dedicated avoidance of the conventional is never allowed to degenerate into the eccentric.

Linda, the heroine of *Holiday* (1928), is a rich girl stifled by her family's stuffy conventionality: her favourite friends are a decorously crazy couple called Nick and Susan Potter ('They get more fun out of nothing than anyone I know'). The part of Nick Potter was based on Barry's friend, Donald Ogden Stewart – who *had* been tapped for Skull and Bones and who played the part himself on the stage. (He later adapted both *Holiday* and *The Philadelphia Story* for the screen, but strayed, as it were, into another scenario and became a Hollywood Communist.) Johnny Case, the hero, falls in love with Linda's snobbish sister Julia without realising that she is an heiress; when he *does* realise this, he wants to go off with her to Europe and 'do nothing' instead of joining her father's business firm, and only Linda sees his point. Again, business is the enemy – of what, is never made quite clear. 'I want to live every whichway, among all kinds – and know them – and understand them – and love them – *that's* what I want!' cries Johnny. Like most of the sympathetic characters in Barry's comedies, he wants to have fun – and fun has nothing to do with making money, only with spending it in a gracious and tasteful way.

The Animal Kindgom (1932) is an ingenious reversal of the standard triangle drama of the period: here it is the wife who is the scheming gold-digger and the mistress who is the under-standing sport. The hero is a publisher who says things like: 'His work is the only true mistress a real artist ever had. When he takes on the world he takes on a whore.' His wife seduces him into publishing trashy novels called *Indian Summer* and

Young Ecstasy for financial gain. His mistress, Daisy Sage, works for fashion magazines but, like Maitland White, wants to 'paint':

> I believe that if I work my eyes out, and my fingers to the bone, some day I may paint. You must be hard with me – no parties – no hell-raising – *work*. And you mustn't let me show until you know I'm ready.

Her friends are a violinist ('Good! – You'll get there, Franc, if you work') and a novelist engaged on a book called *Easy Rider* ('But what does it mean?' 'Good God, must it mean something?').

Daisy Sage is a great Barry heroine: bohemian but monogamous, proud but vulnerable, awesomely intense but never quite abandoning the light touch. She has something in common not only with Tracy Lord of *The Philadelphia Story* (1939) but also with Macaulay Connor in the same play – the cynical reporter for *Destiny* magazine who has published a book of short stories. ('They're so damned beautiful,' Tracy tells him. 'The one called "With the Rich and Mighty" – I think I liked *it* best.') Everything is wrong with the man Tracy thinks she wants to marry: he is a 'man of the people', a careerist, a humourless snob who doesn't believe in having fun. Neither, for much of the play, does Tracy herself, a 'virgin goddess' whose standards of taste and grace are impossibly high. Her sin is to disapprove of her father's embarrassing involvement with a show-girl; her punishment is to believe, erroneously, that while drunk she slept with Macaulay Connor; her reward is remarriage with the rich playboy C. Dexter Haven. The play ends with a crucial exchange between Tracy and her erring father:
'How do I look?'
'Like a queen – like a goddess.'
'Do you know how I feel?'
'How?'
'Like a human – like a human being!'
Barry was exceptionally happily married, with two sons, but the father-daughter relationship for some reason obsessed him. It is prominent in *Hotel Universe*, basic to *The Philadelphia Story*

and dominant in the play he was working on when he died, aged fifty-three, in 1949. *Second Threshold* was posthumously performed in a version completed by Robert E. Sherwood; it is printed here as Barry left it. Interesting, imperfect, almost painfully personal, it appears to be a study of what would now be called the 'male menopause' but shirks the issue halfway through: the successful, cultured, urbane elderly lawyer is only pretending to be suffering from a crisis of confidence. His aim is to prevent his devoted but over-intellectual daughter, significantly named Miranda, from marrying a 'boring' Englishman old enough to be her father. The ruse succeeds, and when Miranda falls instead for a young American 'in his mid-twenties, spare, rangy, with a humorous, likeable face, not at all handsome', she is congratulated, like Tracy, on 'joining the human race'.

The incestuous undertones are all the more disturbing for being nervously camouflaged beneath an air of conservative complacency unusual in Barry's work. Johnny Case of *Holiday*, who refused to be 'made over' in the image of Wall Street, has matured into Josiah Brook of *Second Threshold*, bitterly aware that the civilised values he has lived for are threatened by the horrors of the modern world. It only takes a generation for cheeky hedonism to harden into peevish reaction.

Why did Barry apparently long, like Mr Dearth in *Dear Brutus*, for a 'dream daughter' he never had? I think the answer is that he had fallen in love with his own composite heroine – Linda, Daisy, Tracy, Miranda – daring, chaste, highly bred, independent, fastidiously witty and fundamentally decent: the image so potently purveyed by the personality of Katharine Hepburn. And the only possible relationship with this ideal creation would be that of a proud father gazing, as into a magic mirror, at his beautiful, arrogant, momentarily rebellious but ultimately obedient child.

1975

PART THREE
PEOPLE AND PLACES

ADA LEVERSON

M Y GRANDMOTHER ADA LEVERSON IMAGINED THAT THE height of bliss would be to sit in a theatre listening to her own dialogue spoken by 'real live actors', and much of her life was spent in trying to finish a play. It was always the same play, but as time drew level with her inspiration and threatened to leave it behind, the characters and dialogue had every so often to be brought up to date by radical alteration before the final curtain was reached. Three separate versions survive: they may be seen to correspond with adequate fidelity to the three main 'acts' in the drama of her life. The name of her play was *The Triflers*.

The first version belongs to the 1890s and was conceived as a vehicle for her favourite performer, Charles Hawtrey. She had acquired the English rights in a successful French comedy which satirised the pose of decadence in *fin-de-siècle* society and centred on a ludicrously morbid suicide-pact. Her adaptation was full of paradoxical epigrams in the manner of Oscar Wilde, with five acts, a duke and a duchess among the leading parts and a scene set in a conservatory during a ball. This reflects her happiest period, for which she is most often remembered – as an unconventional but respectable literary hostess contributing witty sketches and parodies to fashionable magazines, the dazzled disciple of Wilde who was to prove herself, during and after his disgrace, a loyal and courageous friend.

She was thirty-eight when Wilde died in 1900, and the next twenty years brought other sadnesses. Her marriage ended in separation; her friends became fewer; she suffered from ill health and was harassed by money worries. Yet during this period (between 1907 and 1916) she produced six novels in which the originality of her sense of the ridiculous finds full expression. She hated writing them and only did so to please her publisher, Grant Richards, with whom, at the time, she was in love. The echoes of Wilde have gone, to be replaced by a celebration of inconsequence even more extreme than his, which nonetheless seems to be more deeply rooted in reality. This is the tone of the second version of *The Triflers*, which was trimmed down to four acts, with an added farcical sub-plot lifted from an unpublished short story of hers about a man whose handwriting is so illegible that it causes endless confusion. Unhappily in love, he innocently confides by letter to a married female friend: 'I am sick of dancing attendance on that woman and can bear it no more. She is frivolous and heartless, and I shall go to Norway to fish as soon as I can get a pal to go too.' The recipient cannot make out a word of this, but her husband finds the note and reads the passage as: 'You are the soul of my existence, you dear woman, and our love is our life. He is frivolous and hateful and we may – *word indecipherable* – tell the fool to go hang.' To save her marriage from his furious threats of divorce, the bewildered wife engages a handwriting expert to clear up the mystery, but he complicates matters still further with a third interpretation: 'I'm quick at making verses and have finished the play in an hour. It is possible and probable that I shall bring it out as soon as I can get a man to go shares.'

After the First World War, Ada Leverson's company was sought by a younger generation of gifted men (Osbert and Sacheverell Sitwell, Harold and Willie Acton, Ronald Firbank, Raymond Mortimer) who saw her as an intriguing survivor from the faded *Yellow Book* past. Encouraged by these, she published a slim volume containing her reminiscences of Wilde and his letters to her, for the third time achieving a modest celebrity as the faithful friend whom he had called 'the Sphinx'. (When Wyndham Lewis put her in *The Apes of God* as 'the Sib' she was the only target of his satirical malice to be clearly delighted, and even flattered, by the attention.) The last version of *The Triflers* was written in the 1920s as a possible 'come-back' for the ageing star, Mrs Patrick Campbell. It now had only three acts, butler and footmen had been replaced by the telephone, and the ducal conservatory had become a streamlined modern interior belonging to a young man called the Honourable 'Daisy' Vane. 'Decorations by Bakst,' the stage directions read. 'Pictures by Wyndham Lewis, Picasso and Gauguin. Music by Goosens and Stravinksy. Books by Wyndham Lewis, Proust, Stephen Hudson, T. S. Eliot, Osbert Sitwell and Zola.' But she still couldn't *quite* make the last act long enough, and when she died in 1933 she left *The Triflers* incomplete.

I was nine years old at the time, and was not immediately told of her death. I remember asking after her in an autumn garden and my mother breaking the news. For me it was the first time that the idea of death could be realised as the protracted absence of a member of my own small circle. Before the message reached my brain, tears had spurted out of my eyes. I could not understand how my mother had been able to travel up to London to nurse the patient, make arrangements for the funeral, and be otherwise absorbed, without my having known anything about it. I felt insecure; after an interval I began to miss my grandmother in a straightforward way, and continued to do so until grief was subsumed in curiosity and pride. It is possible that in that garden, nearly fifty years ago, my memories of Ada Leverson, few but vivid, shifted from chaos into the acceptable form in which they have been ever since preserved.

I saw later that in old age she must have been something of a trial to her friends and family, however devoted they may have been in theory, but nothing ever diminished her attraction for children, who responded with enraptured recognition to her dedicated frivolity and shared her serious dread of boredom. She had grown very deaf; she was totally and dangerously impractical (could not, as used to be said, 'boil a kettle'); although she had once been rich, she was now invariably in debt (having, as also used to be said, 'absolutely no money-sense whatsoever'); she was both gently demanding and stubbornly independent: yet she always managed to seduce into her orbit people who were happy to wait on her. Her arrivals to stay with my parents in Wiltshire were looked forward to by the whole household ('Isn't it funny the way the place seems to cheer up when Mrs Leverson comes on a visit?'), although they were seldom free from worry and sometimes contained an element of slapstick. My grandmother never succeeded in leaving the train at the station where she was expected and, engrossed in a book ('my little Henry James') or deep in a doze, would be carried triumphantly beyond it. Whoever had driven

in to meet her would then have to return, depressed by a sense
of anti-climax, to await a panic-stricken telephone call from
Devizes or somewhere even further along the Great Western
Railway line. On one famous occasion, a much longer time
than usual had elapsed while the telephone remained silent
and the anxiety of my parents was becoming acute. At last it
rang. 'Penzance speaking,' said a distant voice. 'Sorry to trouble
you, but there's a party here says she's for Hungerford.'

In this context, 'party' meant a funny old lady, but it was a
suitable term for my grandmother, who carried an atmosphere
of festivity around with her. She loved popular tunes and at
any period of her life would be 'mad about' some contemporary
hit – from *The Belle of New York*, *The Merry Widow*, *Hello Ragtime!*
or the early Noël Coward revues. Unable to read music, she
played the piano by ear in an enjoyably slapdash way, and
when she came to stay the house would be filled with the sound
of these irresponsible melodies, which worked on one's spirits
like the concept of a cocktail. At the time of my infancy there
had been a currently successful song with a repetitive rhythmic
refrain: 'You are my *Chili*-Bom-Bom! My *Chili*-Bom-Bom! My
Chili-Bom-Bom!' Beguiled by its sprightly nonsense, she got it
'on the brain' and would sing it to amuse me while dancing me
up and down on her lap, so that I came to identify the comical
syllables with her desirable presence and, when I wished to
indicate her, would babble 'A-Bom-Bom!' This stuck, for my
brother and myself, as her official name, solving the problem
of how to skirt round 'Grandmother' (which would have irri-
tated her as a tactless reminder of her age) or any of its diminu-
tives (which would have offended her by their sentimental
whimsy; she had forbidden my mother ever to call her 'Mummy'
because of its disagreeable association with burial customs in
ancient Egypt).

These visits never lasted long; I'm afraid they bored her, for
her departure always seemed to take place sooner than had
been planned. She disliked country life, and would almost
immediately succumb to nostalgia for her room at the Washington Hotel in Curzon Street, for the cat awaiting her there, for
the amusement of metropolitan gossip, for the reassurance of
proximity to Hatchards in Piccadilly and for the stimulation of

a possible meeting with Osbert Sitwell, the object of her love. But before she left, a ceremony would have taken place, the recollection of which evokes her personality for me now as potently as ever.

She would read aloud to my brother and me from the *Alice* books – her favourites as well as ours. This was the greatest of treats but, like most pleasures in youth, cruelly brief: indeed, it was the very intensity of the enjoyment it gave all three of us which set a limit to its duration. In this case, it was not the children who ruined their own fun by getting 'over-excited' but the grown-up who soon became physically incapable of continuing, silenced by an uncontrollable *fou rire*. Some touch of inspired inconsequence, of exquisite absurdity in Lewis Carroll's text would prove too much for my grandmother. Her short, square body, clothed from neck to ankles in shiny black satin, would start to shake convulsively, rocking the chair we leant on; the wide black brim of the picture hat, worn even indoors over her brightly-dyed golden hair, would quiver in sympathy, then rakishly dip over her whitened face, by now convulsed and weeping in an ecstatic agony of soundless mirth. Then the pale-framed spectacles would slip off her nose to become dangerously entangled with the long necklace of amber beads on her heaving bosom; the clasp of her handbag would burst open, and an overspill of leather spectacle-case, loose cigarettes, cologne-scented handkerchief, powderpuff and mirrored compact, eventually followed by *Alice* itself, would slowly slither from her lap to the ground. The suddenness, the totality of this collapse from adult responsibility into the childish abandon of wildly infectious laughter made her seem to belong to a third world ruled by magic and jokes. The episode had the arbitrary unreason and challenging glamour of a miraculous transformation scene: it was as if we had gained entry into the book she had been reading from, privileged to penetrate beyond the mystery of print, and in a wonderland through the looking-glass had been comfortably confronted by a benign domestic monster, familiar as the nursery fender, yet foreign as the sphinx.

1982

THE PEARLY KING

'COME INTO MY CRYSTAL PALACE!' SAID NORMAN HARTNELL at the entrance of his *maison de couture* in Bruton Street, Mayfair. He has been there since 1935, and the decor has remained more or less unchanged: green marble, columns of faceted mirror-glass, Negro lampstands and a galaxy of chandeliers. It is indeed a palace – suitable setting for a man who has triumphantly imposed his personal fantasies of extravagant femininity on two generations of tweedy English ladies.

The ground floor is occupied by the *petit salon*, selling semi-couture and ready-to-wear – a fairly recent innovation. But it is on the first floor, dedicated to *haute couture*, that the essential Hartnell begins. The glass door to the splendid *salon* is patterned with stars: 'We added them on because ladies used to bump their noses against the transparent glass. They did, you know, they were very silly.'

Mr Hartnell, who is sixty-seven, has a house in Windsor Forest but sometimes sleeps at his flat on the third floor in Bruton Street. 'Six charwomen arrive in the morning and have the pleasure of cooking the boss's breakfast! Come upstairs – young whippersnappers like ourselves don't need the lift. The second floor is let to the hairdresser Alexandre de Paris – which means Alexander of Paris. Here's our ugly little Gentlemen's. I love old mahogany surrounds, don't you? They make charming photo frames.'

Pictures hang by the stairs. 'This is a souvenir of the Queen Mother's visit to Paris in 1938 – I made her a trousseau all in white. This is my French decoration, given me after the Queen Mother's visit by the French Government – which proves what large-hearted artists they are. This is my MVO – *two* Elizabeth signatures, you see, rather nice. This is a portrait of me in levee dress for the Coronation: I look like a sort of male Mona Lisa.'

In his private sitting room, a Winterhalter of the Empress

Eugénie and her ladies in waiting hangs over the fireplace. 'People are always recognising their great-aunts among those ladies. Eugénie is my idol – she and the Empress Elizabeth of Austria. Such a romantic period, with everything sewn on by hand. Girls in tissue paper cuffs literally putting these things on one by one. I always say Worth copied Hartnell in those days.

'Mine's a Cinderella story, you know. Out of the drabbery of Maida Vale, to this. (Though of course I'd been to the University where one's treated like a lord, with servants and everything.) I know that dress designing in this country is still regarded as rather an effete occupation. I'm always getting letters saying "My son is an absolute duffer and I think he'd make a good dress designer." But it's not too bad to end up by dressing a Sovereign, is it? And I'm not talking about a king's wife. A *ruling Sovereign!*

'Most dress designers in London are really expert tailors: Hardy Amies, Digby Morton, Lachasse. I specialise more in clothes for starlight time – when the lamps are low or the chandeliers are glittering. Then you can put *beauty* into clothes! Certainly they can wear their brown twin-sets all day if they want to: but indigenous femininity must be slaked in the romantic hours of the evening. Unfortunately, as we all know, there aren't many occasions now when they can put on lovely long elaborate gorgeous trailing dresses. Even at night these days a little black cocktail dress is considered adequate. People don't mind being seen at the Opera in a soiled twin-set . . .

'I remember when a dinner-jacket was underdressed for a man. It's quite true, you know – they were slack. I was always popping in my imitation diamond studs – ping! ping! and off to a party. People often say to me "You'd have liked to live in the age of brocade and ruffles" but I answer "No, I'd have liked to be twenty in 1900, the late Edwardian period which Cecil Beaton has made his own." The men then were quite the smartest. Now I think men can only be chic in their country clothes. Those ravishing autumn colours – olive green, ginger, sky blue and saffron. *That's* the time, even today, at country-house parties, when ladies can put on evening dress and trail down the broad staircase looking really glamorous.

'In my July Collection I included a replica of a dress I made for Gertie Lawrence thirty years ago. With a little bit of couturier cunning, I revived it to time with the premiere of *Star*. It was almost the only one photographed by the press – and quite the loveliest of the lot. After showing eighty shifts and shapeless caftans, along came this gorgeous garment of linear allure, the colour of lilac, shrouded across the shoulders, with a fishtail of tulle. It was *genuinely* expensive – I'd had the material twelve years, silk tulle which you can't get here. Anyway, it drew nostalgic sighs from all, as well as four millionaires who wanted to buy it for their wives. Which proves there's still a thirst for the shamelessly theatrical yet breathlessly beautiful in *haute couture*.

'Ah, Gertie! I adored that woman so much that I wanted to get away from her! She made me *ill* with fascination, I couldn't be in her presence. But she wasn't all sugar and spice, you know. No, Gertie was like a little serpent: she would tremble with temper and shiver with chic! (I say, that's rather good!) But she was so delicious, nobody minded.

'People always ask the question: do you only sell one of each model? Of course we don't. The Collections cost thousands, and each model is there to be copied by as many women as want to buy it. Then they ask: but what if two of them go to the same party in the same dress? (This happened once to me with Evelyn Laye and Bebe Daniels – but they both looked so lovely it didn't matter!) Of course, those who look the best do win. But what comforts the others is that everybody knows they've paid a snobby price for this somewhat exclusive dress. Of course it's quite a different matter with dresses designed by Royal Command for certain ladies we know of. And if by chance one of these ladies should choose a model from the Collection, that model is instantly eliminated. The Queen knows that.

'I often meet people at parties who say "I love your shop but never dare come in because I don't know anybody there." I tell them it's only a shop, you can come in and look round and say there's nothing exactly *me*. I've strolled round both Cartier's and Woolworth's without a personal introduction to the ladies and gentlemen of the staff. The ladies here will be delighted to see any old soul.

'Upstairs we have Madame Vera, the Directrice, and three vendeuses – plus one to look after the *petit salon* (when she isn't studying the racing form!). We used to have six permanent mannequins sitting in the *cabine* all the year round, but now we've only two. We engage freelance models for the Collections. The danger is if you get someone looking like Marilyn Monroe you're inclined to dress them to their own type. You plod away at a Collection – say, 100 dresses. We designers over here have to think of our customers – but sometimes the pencil slips over the drawing-board and you design something regardless and *that* is the artist's outlet for self-expression.

'One's guided a lot by the new materials. Going through thousands of patterns is a strenuous job and somewhat heartache-making because the most beautiful are often unwearable and always the most costly. Feelings are hurt when the loveliest aren't ordered – it's the same for me when the loveliest dresses in my Collection are passed over for a little navy blue coat and skirt. I'm sick to death of the saying "Elegance is utter simplicity", I think it's a hoodwink. Some designers just lack the inventiveness to make it *non*-simple. Of course, for that you've got to get the expert fingers. How can you put all this work – fitters, girls, time and imagination – into a ready-to-wear dress some woman wants to buy in a few minutes for a few pounds?

'In October I'll be choosing the materials for my show next January. Then I wait for the deliveries from Paris. All of us in London suffered in the summer from the strikes in France. Deliveries were late, sometimes thirty-six hours before the opening. I was held up working on an extravagant ensemble of champagne pink skirt, top embroidered in rubies and diamonds, long champagne pink evening coat with elbow-length cuffs of white mink. We lacked a yard of pink material to make one sleeve, therefore the whole get-up could not be shown. All that beauty sacrificed for one yard of stuff! A whole pile of it was placed on approval in Paris with one of the great couturiers. That explains itself. Wouldn't let it go, you see.'

Mr Hartnell was approached by a middle-aged man with a military moustache: 'Captain' Mitchison, who helps him run the business. 'Sorry to interrupt, but my young niece, Clare, wants advice about her new flat. She's got a blue carpet and needs help with the wallpaper. The young are impatient.'

'Tell her to try Sanderson's – they have bales and bales of lovely lilac.'

'You tell her – I don't want to be responsible if it's a failure.'

While his employer good-naturedly obeyed, Mitchison explained that he is not really a captain. 'It's only the Old Gentleman calls me that: I worked in uniform the first six months after the war, and never got rid of the name. Oh, we've all been here for ages. The baby of the family, Jack the electrician, has been here twenty years. The van driver for thirty. The housekeeper came before the war – she was an ARP girl in the basement shelters. Now she does the canteen – if anybody's sick or faints, shout for Flo! Mrs Price has been secretary since the war. Miss Mills in the counting-house is retiring in October after thirty-four years, and by God we can't replace her! People you never see, but all so fantastically loyal! One girl's retiring soon after forty-four years, came here straight from school. Alice the fitter, a dear old soul, she's over retiring age and she said, "I must retire soon or I'll have nothing to retire *to*!" '

Mr Hartnell returned. 'The only woman who's ever been rude to me was Marlene. I used to alter her Jean Louis clothes for nothing at the Café de Paris. Then I was asked to make her a white mink coat, *yards* long, for free – they thought I needed the publicity. I said sorry, I couldn't afford it. That evening I saw her at her show talking to some dirty little girls. Somebody said, "This is Norman" and she said, "Is it really?" and walked straight into her dressing room. But I still think she's a wonderful performer. Isn't that big of me?

'The other day we had a visit from Princess Muna – oh, *very* royal! She just sat there and said nothing. Everybody felt so sorry for me!'

'She can talk all right,' said Mitchison, 'because I met her at a party and she gave me a hell of a rocket. Said she came in here wanting a wedding dress and the vendeuse said, "We're too busy." '

'As for fashion editors – well we all know about them, don't we? Do you remember Carmel Snow, who was Editor of *Harper's*? She always used to sleep through the Collections. I was determined to wake her up one day. We were showing a wedding dress (it might have done for Princess Muna!) called Scylla and Charybdis or something, so at the last moment I changed the name to *Snow* on Mount *Carmel*. When she heard it bellowed out she *did* wake up for a minute or two.

'I could *strangle* some of these students who bring in useless sketches! Belts hanging down low, tiny little skirts, models squatting with legs apart. I may be rather a square house, but why waste my time? I couldn't possibly send those to certain ladies we know of, certain Royal ladies, could I?

'Tonight's my Last Supper – tomorrow I swish down to Forest Mere to starve for ten days. I want to be left alone, I want to be Garbo. They said "We're giving you a room facing the lake." I don't give a fig where I face – I'd face the drainpipe. I rang up Heywood Hill for *Emerald and Nancy* but they say it's out of print so I'm taking Madge Garland's book on the 1930s, something called *Life With Queen Victoria*, which sounds just my cup of tea, and stacks and stacks of Ouida and Elinor Glyn.

'I used to employ nearly 400 people, now it's down to 250. There just aren't the rich people nowadays so one doesn't need the staff. And even if I did, I couldn't get them. Girls these days don't want to sew on sequins till they go cross-eyed when they can work in factories with *Music While You Work* and the boys. Most of them live in the suburbs – ghost cities where they can walk to a factory in ten minutes. I sometimes wonder if there will be any *haute couture* ten years from now: a woman hasn't time for five or six interminable fittings when she needs a dinner dress to wear that night and a tweed suit for the weekend.'

'Every New Year's Eve we have a jolly party,' said Mitchison, 'then wake up the next day to realise that during the coming year our outgoings will be from £120,000 to £150,000. This house is our image. It's not a question of *if* we lose on the image, but how much. The image has to be paid for by the sidelines, like ready-to-wear. We have a little factory in the East End for that. Stockings, handbags, costume jewellery – all very reasonably priced, but you can't sell expensive stuff nowadays.'

'And we do a scent called *In Love*,' said Mr Hartnell. 'Nice name, isn't it?'

'But the profit has to come from the couture,' said Mitchison, 'and we can't ask what we should for that.'

'No,' said Mr Hartnell. 'Every woman who comes in for a dress is hard as a nailfile whether you're friends, darling, when she's pickled at parties or not. And if clothes are well made, they last too long from our point of view. The other day a lady brought in a sapphire blue dress and magenta coat I'd made for her in 1936. The style was perfect, it hadn't faded and not a *bead* was off. But she was livid because after hanging in her cupboard for over thirty years it had dropped a quarter of an inch!'

1968

MOTHER AND SON

'YOU KNOW THE STORY, DON'T YOU? IT'S REALLY RATHER interesting. I married my art teacher, Ernest Entwistle. He fell in love with me at first sight. I was learning fashion drawing actually, dear – but I was already an artist, you see. I came from a very happy home, surrounded by art and music and all that. Florence Vivienne Mellish was my name. I was one of eleven children – rather amusing, isn't it? Well, I was in no hurry to marry, but Ernest wouldn't take no for an answer, so I said, "I'll marry you on one condition only, and that is that for a year after the wedding I do nothing at all but study art." Well, he agreed of course so I gave in and we were married in 1913 and we had our Golden Wedding in 1963 and then he decided to go over the rainbow and that was that.

'During the first year I became crazy about the miniatures in the Wallace Collection. I said to my husband: "You know about drawing but I know about colour," and then I painted my first miniature. I've still got it. So I did a lot of them and later I used to colour enormous enlargements of photographs of film stars to put outside the cinemas. Then we had two sons. Tony was always very brilliant as a little boy. He went to the Philological School in Marylebone Road – it's a grammar school now but it was very nice then – and he left when he was just under fifteen with an "excellent" in every subject. He's always been brilliant at everything, isn't it terrible? That's why I wasn't at all unhappy when he went off forever in 1957 because I know that wherever he is he'll always be at the very top of his profession.

'Well, when he left school he took some lessons in art in my husband's studio and then he got interested in photography. It was more the equipment that intrigued him at first, I think. So I bought him an old Kodak camera and some lights and then, of course, he was very far-seeing, he found one room to let as a studio for photography. He took his first portrait when he was fifteen and he signed it Antony Roger, because that was his name, Antony Roger Entwistle. Then he had a bit of luck because he met Vivien Leigh just when she had first made her name in *The Mask of Virtue* – she was so lovely then, you've no idea – and his picture of her became famous all over the world. So he went ahead like that.

'I used to do his re-touching for him, he wasn't very good at that. We created a sort of family firm and called it Twentieth Century Studios. We started in Sackville Street and then we moved to Orchard Street opposite Selfridge's Food Store. Then one weekend he phoned to say he wasn't well and he had a sitting and would I go round and help – and that's how I took my first professional picture. This was in 1938 and I was fifty-one. Yes, dear, I'll be eighty-four next July, and you can say I'm still working as hard as ever. I live in my mind, you see, and my body's got to respond! Well, people seemed to like my work so I went on and I called myself by my middle name, which is Vivienne, and Tony and I became rivals. I had a friendship with Beatrice Lillie, we'd lived near her in St John's Wood, and she sat for me and the picture was a full page in the *Tatler* and from then on I never looked back. My son was very angry, well, you can't blame him.

'Then unfortunately he got very friendly with a family who wanted him to branch out on his own. He was still very young and you know what it's like sometimes with young men and older women. . . This was a very sad part of my life and of his. When he opened his studio at Cleveland Row in 1939 he adopted the name of Antony Beauchamp. I didn't pay much notice to it, I didn't really care. He changed his name by deed poll, you know, I suppose he thought it would shock me, but I never alluded to it, not once. Then one morning at three o'clock the phone went and a voice said "Mother," and I thought it was Clive, that's the other one, but he said, "No, it's Tony, I'm so unhappy Mother dear, I can't tell you the trouble I ran into." So I said "Come back," and he came back and we never, never discussed it from that day on.

'Now of course the war was coming. As soon as I'd married we'd had one war, and now we had another. Tony never grumbled. He went off to Sandhurst and got his Commission and he had a brilliant war: as you know, he became the Official War Artist to the 14th Army. "I didn't take glamour pictures in Burma, Mother dear," he said, "I took the bloody sights!" He was always going up, Tony, and I believe he's still going up . . . I haven't said much about Clive, have I? He's brilliant too, the same brilliance keeps on coming through the family all the time, isn't it awful? He came to me one day – he knew I could keep a secret – and he told me he'd designed a jet engine. Then he went down to Farnborough and he came back and he said, "Would you believe it, Whittle's onto it already!" You wouldn't believe it, would you? Yes, he designed some rocket or other which they used as a secret weapon, but of course he never got any credit for it because it was secret, you see, dear. He'd already made his name as an architect and got very friendly with Corbusier, who praised him to the skies. He designed the biggest tractor in the world – I always think that sounds like Gracie Fields! – for two men to take right across the Sahara in two weeks. And he designed the second largest building for the World Fair. Unfortunately that World Fair was not a success and they went broke, but he got enormous publicity for it and it was a nice thing to do. *His* son is brilliant too, he's a Balliol man, he got a Second in Persian and a Second in Arabic and now he's a dealer in antiques, rather amusing, isn't it?

'Well, to go back to the war days, I did wvs work for a bit and then I said, "I *must* start photography again!" In a mad moment I took a darling little studio in Hamilton Mews, so badly bombed I can't tell you, they gave me six months credit and I paid it all in four. My husband always used to joke that one day I'd come to him and say, "I've seen a To Let sign on Buckingham Palace!" So then I made my name straight away all over again. Then my *husband* went mad and saw 23 Hertford Street and insisted on getting that. Well, one day the phone rang and my assistant said, "Mrs Entwistle, it's Tony!" I said, "Where are you?" and he said, "At Paddington Station!" After four years, just like that. So he moved in and of course, being Tony, he took over.

Well, he went on, he was very handsome of course, all the glamour girls fell for him. He never took a man – did you notice, dear? I like taking the glamour girls but I like taking men too.

I study their faces, you see. My life has all been in what I call *faces*. I used to say to my husband, "Tony at his best, I couldn't take one as good, but at his worst, I couldn't take one as terrible!" My husband would say that my average was Tony's best, but I'd tell him not to be sillly!

'I'd stand opposite a Rembrandt all day and I'd think, "Now why did he put that little bit of green just there?" Then when I came to study my lighting I understood what he was doing. I can soften what I want to and delete what I want to at the re-touching stage, but the rest has to be done by lighting. When Cecil Beaton came to be taken I said, "My knees are trembling, you know," and he said, "Whatever for?" and I said, "You know what I'm up to and the others don't!" He laughed. He was wearing such ridiculous clothes! I do like taking men but I thought it so sad to come in a black city gent's suit and a stiff white collar . . .

'I've done seven prime ministers, you know. Attlee, of course. Eden used my picture in his election. Then out of the blue there was a phone call from Mr Macmillan's secretary: "Would Madame Vivienne go to Downing Street at four on Wednesday to photograph the PM?" Well, I never go out. So he had to come to me here at Adam and Eve Mews. He told me he'd flown Karsh of Ottawa over specially to photograph him but the pictures had been disappointing. Somehow the press must have got hold of this because they rang me for a quote and I did say I thought his lighting could be rather harsh; well, I asked for that, because the next day they had great headlines saying "Viv harsh about Karsh"! I was so upset, I rang Chequers at once and Lady Dorothy answered (she had a very distinctive voice) and she said, "Oh, we never bother about what the papers say!" Sarah, my daughter-in-law said, "Don't worry, darling, it's fantastic publicity!" She had the actress's point of view, I suppose. Then when I was asked to go to the Foreign Office to do Lord Home, as he was then, I said, "Oh dear, we can't keep on saying no," so I went. He was sitting behind an empty desk and I said, "You don't look as if you ever do any work here," so the secretary brought some papers, but he said, "Take them away, they're all top secret!" I said, "Lord Home, I promise you the writing won't come out!" In between I took

Heath, he was very bright and breezy, I think he's matured since then and gone *into* himself. Then Wilson got in. He was rather shy and blinked terribly, isn't that amusing? But when people ask me who's the most wonderful person I've photographed, I always say first Sir Winston Churchill and then Vivien Leigh. As you know, in 1949 Sir Winston became Tony's father-in-law.

'Tony knew Sarah slightly before the war, she came to be photographed. He couldn't bear her at first, didn't like her at *all*, isn't it amusing? Then she came back and one day he said to me, "I've got very friendly with Sarah Churchill, Mother dear, I saw her in a very different light at the Dorchester the other night." It's my belief she'd been in love with him all along! They all were. Sarah I adore. They were very happy together at first but somehow things went wrong. She branched away on her own, she had her own career as an actress and he of course had his. He went into film production, you know, and he had one all ready to go, he'd got all the stars and everything, and then an American backer – I'd better not mention his name – let him down at the last moment. Tony just couldn't take any more and he swallowed all his sleeping pills. He was only thirty-nine . . . Sarah was marvellous to me. To this day she calls me her mother-in-law and she won't be photographed by anybody else.

'Tony left all his photographs to me – and then Sarah officially did, as she was the next of kin. I'm not really a believer in spiritualism – I wouldn't try to get into touch with him – but I don't believe in life finishing. I think we go on. To me, Tony went straight on. He couldn't help it. He took his own life, I know that, but I think that's a very plucky thing to do. We were always very friendly, very near to each other, which is rare for a mother and son. Although we had that argument, I know it wasn't his fault. I'm a very proud mother. He wrote me fabulous letters: just before he was going off to war, such pages and pages pouring out his admiration and love for me. And the last letter he wrote before he went away for good was to me. I look at him sometimes – at one of the pictures I took of him – and I think: "Why don't you help me? What shall I do with all the lovely photographs you left behind?" I've started a book about him. It's called *My Son, My Son*. Isn't it a lovely title? He wrote one himself, you know, *Focus on Fame*; it came out after his death. And I'm also writing the story of my own life. A lot of sorrow, a lot of tragedy, a lot of laughter and a lot of love: that's the theme. Two very charming men who are very brilliant at writing are helping me with it; I met them at Brighton, where I have a dear little Gothic house. It's been accepted by Leslie Frewin who's bringing it out in the autumn. I think it will interest people because it is such an extraordinary story, isn't it? I'm calling that one *Portrait by Vivienne* – again, a lovely title. I'm rather good at thinking up titles. Why don't you call the article you're writing about me "Mother and Son"?'

1971

Camera club

EVERY OTHER FRIDAY EVENING, THE SELSDON CAMERA CLUB meets at the local Guide Hut for a portrait session. 'Come on in, here's where we do the masterpieces. We've got a blonde model laid on for tonight and we're going to try some high-key work on her.'

Round the the walls of a narrow room were notices about the Chaffinch, Kingfisher, Swallow and Canary Patrols, and a picture of Princess Anne. The club has fifty-four members, of whom fourteen were present: all men except for Mrs Richardson. 'My husband and I are both members. It's a very pleasant club, not one of the big ones but a *friendly* club. I'm sure a lot of people join for social reasons.' Indeed, three or four of the members do not even possess cameras: 'They just enjoy themselves.'

Several of the men were smoking pipes. Brian Miller, the secretary, owns a dental laboratory. Reg Holdstock, the programme secretary, is a retired policeman. Ken Hubbard, the chairman, works in motor insurance. Patrick Dempsey and Lawrence Cutler are still at school. Pat Jenkins is foreman at a vacuum-cleaner factory: he had come to the session but had forgotten to bring any film. 'I live in Leatherhead and Alf Bird over there lives in Epsom, but we prefer the atmosphere at the Selsdon C.C.'

The guest was John Hunnex, ARPS, a freelance photographer very popular with camera clubs as lecturer and judge. 'When we have an evening with John I always put Bring Your Late Night Passes on the programme,' said Reg. 'Because once he starts talking he never stops. He's a real entertainment, has us in fits.'

'There are so many camera clubs now I could virtually go out every night of the year, Saturdays included,' said Hunnex. 'In the old days of box cameras, people thought photography was black magic. But now you're getting cheap equipment, cameras with built-in light meters, pre-set irises and all that nonsense, and they find it's much simpler. Then they like to feel they're learning the little tips. Trouble is, they all copy each other.'

The model was perched on a stool in front of a pale green backcloth and surrounded by lighting equipment: flood, fill-in, spot, snoot. While each member photographed her in turn, Hunnex kept up a vivacious commentary. If the matter was sometimes incoherent, the manner generated an atmosphere of excitement, of shared activity in an artificial crisis, which soon spread round the group.

'Who hasn't been? Who's the next victim? Have you all gone shy? Surely not! . . . All right – Jan, is it? Head to me, darling, and drop your chin, you're giving too much chin. There she is, she looks gorgeous, better even than I do . . . Not too close or you'll burn her to death. Not too far or you'll get that dead look in the eye . . . Never touch the model because some people don't like being touched. I don't mean *touch*, I mean pull . . . Wet your lips, darling. Don't forget, boys, keep asking them to wet their lips . . . Gorgeous, gorgeous . . . See what happened? Soon as she focused her eyes on my hand she forgot she was being photographed and you get a nice natural pose. You've got to use these tricks because if you don't cheat you can't win . . . '

'I've got an itchy nose,' said Jan.

'All right, give her a rest now. Everything stops for tea.'

While Mrs Richardson produced tea and biscuits, the members discussed equipment: 'This is where you get the quality, boy. You'll never get quality with what you're carrying. With me it's Kodak all the way. Except for the colour. Then give me Agfa any day.'

'The new Ektachrome's not so good in my opinion. It goes off badly at slow speeds.'

'I only use Ektachrome Professional – that is, when I can get it.'

'When people mention Lindhof to me, ooh, it winds me up. This camera went for a burton at Guildford Cathedral . . . '

'The value of the cameras at our club is estimated at about, what? £12,000?' said Pat Jenkins. 'I don't know where they get all the money from.'

Most of the members own at least two cameras, a tripod and various lenses: zoom, wide-angle, telescopic. Pat Dempsey, the youngest member, spent over £100 on his equipment, much of it second-hand. 'I joined the club for the competition,' he said. 'I needed it to improve my work. You get tired of just snap-taking, don't you? I've done *some* professional work – technical stuff. But I don't know . . . for one thing, it's very badly paid.'

It is a mistake to look upon the amateur as an unsuccessful professional: his aims and approach are totally different. If the professional's attitude towards the amateur is likely to be one of amused condescension, that of the amateur to the professional is even less complimentary – a blank indifference. 'I never heard any particular name come up that we worship or anything,' said Alf Bird. 'It's more the equipment, I think, that gets worshipped.'

'I think a good amateur will always beat a professional, if you take them in relativity,' said Pat Jenkins. 'He has the time to do it in, less of a rat race. Look at Cecil Beaton. I think his pictures are shocking. Those Royal portraits, and that – so stereotyped. You could turn your back on it and still know where everyone was standing. Now take our friend at the Dorking C.C., Sir George Pollock and his abstracts – they're the best in the world.'

Sir George Pollock specialises in 'vitrographs' – large colour photographs exploiting the prismatic effect of light through glass. Inspired by a visit to Murano, he gave up a legal career to concentrate on this, and recently shared an exhibition at the London Camera Club with his wife. Lady Pollock (also a member of the Dorking and Croydon clubs) works in black and white; her subjects are more representational, with titles like 'Vortex' and poetic captions: 'Winter having touched these fields . . . The very tomtits perched on the scarecrow (Kisaku).'

'I couldn't make head or tail of the Pollock in this week's A.P.,' said Brian Miller. The *Amateur Photographer* is among the best-known of numerous magazines devoted to the hobby, and usually carries over seventy pages of advertising. The editorial includes news from the camera clubs, articles on technical matters, colour portraits of coyly athletic nudes by Dr Johannes

Sachs, and a column in which 'Ricardo' criticises photographs submitted by readers.

'I sent in a picture of my son and daughter – oh, eight years ago,' said Pat Jenkins. 'You saw it, Reg. Very camera-conscious, very pose-conscious. Didn't hear a thing. Then years later someone came up to me and said there's a picture of yours in the A.P. I said there isn't, you know. But there it was, with one of Ricardo's crits. He tore it to pieces. I wanted to tear him to pieces, the nit. Said it was good for a beginner. Well, so I may have been eight years ago – but today I consider myself an accomplished amateur.'

'Most of us belong to Postal Portfolios,' said Reg. 'It's a good idea for people who don't live near a camera club, but anyway I don't believe you should keep your photographs to yourself. A set of twenty prints goes round three times, by post, and we each criticise the nineteen others. We mark them out of twenty for Technique, Presentation, Composition and Appeal, and each time round we take out our own print and put in a new one. Then the winners are exhibited.'

Jan was back on her stool and Hunnex resumed: 'Now when everyone's happy and the young lady's comfortable – give her a gin and she'll be more comfortable – you must talk to her all the time. Ask her if she has a hobby, anything, even if she's bored she'll give you a sultry look . . . Now this is a very harsh light and the only thing to do – has anyone got some gauze? Tissue paper will do. See how the pores of the skin suddenly soften, a bit less like orange peel. No offence, darling . . . Now here's where this little fellow comes in useful. Anybody who's beginning here tonight, you see exactly what your fill-in light is doing, it's killing that shadow there . . . We can't use a spotlight on the background, we've got to use a flood . . . Now we've got to move Big Bertha here . . . I should relax, darling, you'll screw your neck off . . . This man's got the right idea. Only by trial and error, trial and error . . . Talk to her, Reg. Come on, she's human . . . Jan, your hands, dear. Let's see the shine on the hair and we're away . . . Who shot that? Nobody! Call yourselves photographers . . . '

The lights fused.

'There's a deathly hush in the close tonight,' said Pat Jenkins.

'Most of the portrait people are black-and-white merchants,' said Hunnex while the fuse was being mended. 'They come in to do colour but find that black and white is more of a challenge.'

The Selsdon club has been going for twenty years. It belongs to the Surrey Federation, itself a branch of the Central Association of Photographic Societies, and is thus affiliated to the Photographic Alliance of Great Britain. 'The Association draws up lists of lecturers, judges, and so on, which it submits to us,' said Brian Miller. 'During the summer we mostly have prepared lectures, on tape, from the Kodak people. They're very interesting, but not so amusing as the chaps who come down in the winter.' The 1966–7 winter programme promises lectures in person on such subjects as 'With Rucksacks and Cameras in the Alps', 'The Camera Cannot Lie', 'Composition as a Tool of the Trade', and an invitation to 'Come and let your hair down at your own Christmas Party'.

During the summer, outings are organised to local beauty spots. 'The trouble is with these outings,' said Alf Bird, 'you get so many pictures that look the blinking same.'

'The Surrey Fed. gives us a set subject for the year,' said Brian Miller. 'This year it's Work. It was Animals last year, and the year before it was Feet. That was ambiguous – you could take it as Feat if you wanted to. The winner did both – he sent in a picture of a man walking a tightrope in gumboots! You can win cups for the best picture of the year, the best colour slide, the best colour slide for *beginners* (the competition hotted up, so we had to subdivide it) and the most unusual picture. No, it's not called that – the most *imaginative*. That was won last year by a colour slide of two deckchairs. They had a sort of plastic covering, with the sun shining through . . . '

'Composition's a thing you could argue about all night,' said Reg. 'My criterion is: does it give more *impact*?'

The lights were mended, and Jan was induced to put on a sweater. 'Sorry, dear, we'll have to boil you alive,' said Hunnex.

'John's good for another two hours yet,' said Reg as the members clustered round and the commentary continued.

'Move her about a bit, you're getting about 3000 exposures of the same thing. The judges don't like seeing the same things . . . Not too much of the whites of the eyes; I know they

179

say that's when you start shooting, but it's something you mustn't do . . . And then you get the toning off. You can't see it with the eye, but it absolutely saves you from burning in. You can even go one stage further and move the light in, then you get the shading off . . . That's why I say she's low-key. Not many people can take this lighting . . . See those cheek-bones come to life? Now you need your snoot, what I call glamour lighting . . . Don't smile, darling, just look at him as if you hate him . . . Come on now, bit of pop art. All right, Jan? Bit of the fashion stuff, let's have you in the modern pose with your legs apart . . . You must talk to her, it's absolutely crucial, you won't get the eyes going if you don't talk to her . . . Move in, get that highlight on the cheek . . . *Talk* to her, ask her what she's doing tomorrow night . . . Now it's up to you, come on, keep going, bang, bang . . . One moment, give this gentleman a chance . . . OK boys, off you go, hold tight, start moving, lovely, there you go, to me darling, that's gorgeous, now click, click, click, click, click . . . '

1966

THE IMPERIAL HOTEL,
TORQUAY

BETWEEN SIX AND SEVEN O'CLOCK ON SATURDAY EVENING, THE public rooms of the Imperial Hotel are almost empty; the guests are upstairs changing for dinner; 210 businessmen, in Torquay for a conference, have left that morning; 170 new arrivals have just checked in. A woman in the hall is selling Lifeboat badges: 'You can see the boat through the window, actually. It's just been called out.' Beyond the expanse of glass in the Sun Deck Lounge, the sea looks grey. The girl at the switchboard calls a porter over and says, not very urgently: 'There's a light flashing in the bathroom of 309. Could you do something about it?'

The three TV sets are blank: one for BBC just outside the cardroom, one for ITV in the Princess Lounge, and one for colour in the Haldon Room. This room has been sealed off, engaged for a private cocktail party given by students from emergent nations at South Devon Technical College to say goodbye to their landladies and teachers. An enormous African can be seen making a speech; he wears a dinner jacket and, surprisingly, a skirt, with sandals on his sockless feet.

The deserted Crystal Bar begins to fill with waitresses in short green skirts and frilly pink blouses. Then the guests, dressed for the evening, emerge from the lift and walk down the Long Gallery to the bar. Women in mink stoles pause by the fruit machines and crouch to play. Over drinks before dinner ('From the Trolley – Fine Old Vintage Cognac') hotel friendships are cemented, broken or begun. One lady, sitting alone, very slowly takes cigarettes out of a packet and ranges them in an enormous silver case.

Mr and Mrs Szpiro have struck up conversation with a couple from Sheffield. He is a White Russian; she is French, with a suntan and her leg in plaster. 'I came here to convalesce: it's very pleasant with a broken leg because you don't need to go out of the hotel at all. And then that criminal £50! Not that one wants to go to France with all the students rioting. I see it's starting in London now. My husband's bought a property in Buckinghamshire to retire to, because London's not the same as it was.'

'Yes,' says the lady from Sheffield. 'We came up to town recently for the first time in twelve years, and found it *very* different.

'Hampstead used to be so quiet, but now it's all these Espresso bars and youngsters shouting. *Not* my type . . . '

The Dance and Social Hostess, Mrs 'Phyl' Kitley-Carter, and the Dance Host, George Ramsey, begin to circulate. Both live at the hotel, give dancing lessons during the day, and partner any of the guests who seem to want to dance in the evening. Ramsey has a surprised expression and a very slight facial twitch; Mrs Kitley-Carter has an air of great determination.

'I run everything that's going,' she says. 'Bridge, table-tennis, bingo – better not put bingo, isn't it illegal? I don't want to get the head man into trouble. You meet such interesting people. Lots of youngsters I've introduced to each other have asked me to their weddings. Of course, the clientele has altered, like everywhere else in the world. I mean, the money's in different hands now, you've only got to look around you. Better not put that . . . The success of this hotel is due to the friendliness of the staff. And it comes from the top. Do you understand? I mean Mr Chapman himself. Guests are welcomed by every department. When people come back we always endeavour to give them the same table and remember their names. Of course it's quite impossible to remember everybody: how many people do you imagine come here in one year? So we all have a guest list, and if we see H A beside a name we know that means Here Again. If I don't recognise the face I say something like: "I hope you've got a nice room this time, which is it?" Then I look up the room number on the list and get the name that way.'

It's true that Mr Chapman, the Managing Director, sets a high standard of courtesy and good humour; he bustles past, always busy, always pleasant, smiling at some guests, talking to others, kissing the hands of a favoured few. 'Just heard one of the guests has dropped his electric razor and broken it, so I'm popping home to get him another.'

But there's worse trouble to come. A young man staying at the hotel, who is not wearing evening dress, is intercepted on his way to the bar by two massive CID officers and taken to a small room behind the accounts office. It appears that some extremely valuable jewellery has been reported missing from a bedroom near to his. 'Come on, hand it over,' he is told. But Mr Chapman returns from his nearby villa with the razor in time to rescue the bewildered guest.

'We have these troubles at times,' he explains apologetically. 'In fact we've had three big burglaries within the last month. It's most unfortunate because it always casts suspicion on the staff and the people staying here. I have to protect the interests of all my clients, so it's my responsibility to try and elminate these risks. We have signs up everywhere saying PLEASE DEPOSIT YOUR VALUABLES, but people still seem to think if they lock their little handbags they're safe in their suites.'

News of the robbery reaches the bar and lounge. 'Don't look at me,' says the Dance Host, 'I'm absolutely broke. Haven't the nerve, for another thing!' The young man describes his unpleasant experience with the CID. 'It's your own fault for looking such a scruff,' says the Social Hostess.

Guests start drifting into the dining room. The last to come down are a good-looking couple, smartly dressed as though for St Tropez. Mr Zdravkovic is a Yugoslav by birth, with a business in London and an English wife. 'This is our first holiday in England, because of the travel restrictions, but we're terribly disappointed. It's so dead! We bought a lot of nice clothes with us, but what's the point? Nothing to wear them for. And the meals are so early, just like a boarding-house. We're always missing dinner. When you're paying £12 for a room you expect something better. It's a shame, you work hard all year and look forward to your holiday . . . '

During dinner in the vast restaurant with its blue, gold and silver decor (tridents, fishing-nets and stars), as many as three anniversaries are celebrated by choruses of 'Happy Birthday to You' and 'Dear Old Dutch'. The food is undistinguished; but this weekend is not one of the 'Gastronomicals', for which the hotel is famous.

'We're in our eighth season of international Gastronomic Weekends, with six weekends per season,' says Mr Chapman. 'We invite well-known restaurateurs to come and cook their specialities: we've had chefs from behind the Iron Curtain.' (Last season's brochure lists a Wine and Food Society Weekend, a Belgian Weekend, a Côte d'Azur Weekend, an Italian Weekend, a Val de Loire Weekend and a Lyonnais Weekend.)

'We serve matching wines and give cocktail parties and entertainments. There's an inclusive charge of around 25 guineas. We also run a vey successful Gourmet Club.' The objects of this club are 'to promote the art of Gastronomy and Good Living, to stimulate the appreciation of good food and wine, and promote good fellowship and friendship both in this country and abroad'. For an annual subscription of £1, members receive a pass which entitles them, among other privileges, to 'a special welcome whenever they visit the Imperial, Torquay, or any of the allied Hotels and Restaurants' and the right 'to receive a glass of Champagne, a quarter bottle of wine or a drink of their choice on their arrival at such establishments with the compliments of the management'.

The Imperial is over 100 years old. Sir Lawrence Palk (later Lord Haldon), Chairman of the Torquay Hotels Company, built the hotel in 1863; it was opened three years later. It is still owned by a private company, with six members on the board. 'Of course it was entirely a winter season till the 1920s,' says Mr Chapman. 'Families used to move down after the Lord Mayor's Show in November and stay till April. There were low summer rates between May and October. Then from 1921 the whole pattern of holidaymaking changed throughout Europe. It was no longer the prerogative of the landed gentry. The summer became the season: we're always pretty full from Easter till October.'

Now the Imperial has about eight permanent residents. Mr Rossiter, a glove manufacturer from Leicester, has lived there with his wife for eleven years. 'Then there's our Miss Matthews – she's a member of the old Torquay aristocracy, a great character. Always talking about the footmen her father used to keep.

She has a beautiful old Rolls sitting in the garage, it must be forty years old. Arthur Askey (who's one of our regulars) said he thought all the footmen were under the bonnet!'

Miss Matthews is an elegant figure, dozing over her cigarette in the public rooms, wearing a grey coat and a pretty pink hat. 'People often admire this hat. I bought it last year on the spur of the moment, just saw it in the shop and thought it would be nice with my summer things. Jimmy Savile was staying here – such a polite little boy. (I say little, he must be in his forties. But I'm told he's very good to his mother.) He said to me: "Can I borrow your hat?" Oh dear, what *would* people have said seeing him out at the 400 Club wearing my hat! He had two sixpences in his hand, he was going to play those what d'you call 'em machines and he said: "If I win, I'll give you the lot!" Of course he didn't win . . . A very well brought-up little boy.

'This hotel changed management in the last war, it wasn't quite so commercial before. Mr Hore, the previous manager, had a very nice wife. She was a housemaid at the hotel before she married, but I always remember my father telling me what a good little woman she was. He said she was the making of Mr Hore. You see, I think a five-star hotel (which this is) should be *perfect*. I've travelled a lot, and I know. The Royal Bath in Bournemouth, the Polygon in Southampton – I've known them all . . . '

'When I got here in 1939,' says Mr Chapman, 'the hotel had just been requisitioned and was entirely empty. It had gone through a difficult period in the thirties and was at rather a low ebb. I found a shell, with no people and no furniture, so I started from scratch. During the war we had a policy of giving a holiday to as many people as possible; we accommodated three dozen RAF officers at 3½ guineas a week, and thus avoided being requisitioned a second time. It had been very old-fashioned, both in concept and in furniture – brass bedsteads and so on. We modernised the whole of the exterior, and increased the size from 160 beds to nearly 300. We employ a staff of between 200 and 250, which is augmented in the season.'

*

In the accounts office, there is a Long Service Roll of Honour: a board listing employees of over twenty years' standing. 'I believe the staff is the hotel's greatest asset,' says Mr Chapman, 'and we endeavour to maintain as permanent a brigade as possible. We train boys so that now we have head waiters and porters who came here when they were young. Scobie, the hall porter, has been here thirty years; one old boy, Cox, more than fifty years. I try to let them feel we have their interests very much at heart. I hope they realise that if they give good service and welcome people here, they stand to gain. We add 12½ per cent to every bill for gratuities, and the whole of this goes to staff, so it's really a profit-sharing business. We've started a club for them with nightly dances and entertainments. They can enjoy the hotel facilities when these are not in use by guests. One hates to lose an old employee as much as a regular client.

'We sell accommodation, food, drink and service. It's not like a factory where you can examine the products before they're offered to the public. Very often our image can be tarnished by a young inexperienced employee. My main problem is to supervise smooth and efficient service. And one's got to be something of a showman – people want entertainment too. I continually try to see what they want, to let them do whatever they feel like without regimentation. This afternoon, as it was raining, we tried to get a bingo game going; but nobody wanted to play, so we left them alone.

'There's a heated seawater swimming-pool. A croquet lawn and miniature golf course. A new squash court, roll curling, tennis. There are people who come here and never go out of the hotel grounds: we've 5½ acres. Many come several times a year. I like people very much: that's one of the most fascinating and rewarding aspects of my occupation. One's not merely dealing with figures, one comes into contact with so many different types. If you look for the good in them, you can get a lot of enjoyment out of a hotelier's life.

'Our clientele varies. In September, October and throughout the winter it's chiefly retired people, elderly folk who don't want to go too far afield. The climate here in winter is comparatively mild – akin to Nice. No fog, very little snow, not *very* high temperatures, but good for sufferers from bronchitis and similar ailments. During the holiday period we get more young people. Parents bring teenagers and children for a holiday. And young couples who can afford it – young executives, shall we say. We're anxious to attract young executives as they'll be our clients in the future.

'A hotelier must have the instincts of a woman, who constantly changes her clothes, her appearance, her style. In the old days we had no bar. It was a hotel for the families of gentlemen. Then we moved to the more liberal Edwardian and inter-war periods, with cocktail bars and orchestras. Now we find some people don't like Victor Sylvester-type dancing, they want more rhythm and sombre lights. So we started a night club, the Commodore, which is also very much appreciated by the local clientele.'

This evening the Commodore has been taken over for a private party, a local 'twenty-firster', but hotel guests are not excluded. In the ballroom upstairs a husband and wife with a teenage daughter have been sitting after dinner in rather gloomy silence, watching the staid waltzing. A young man propels an elderly lady round the floor and leads her attentively back to her seat. Mrs Szpiro, in spite of her broken leg, dances with her husband; afterwards, she kisses him and says: 'Thank you, darling.' George Ramsey and Mrs Kitley-Carter partner the couple from Sheffield to whom they gave a Rumba lesson in the morning.

Then Mrs Kitley-Carter approaches a group of four unattached men. 'Do you want to dance or play cards? I imagine you'd rather dance. There's a sweet young thing sitting only a few tables away.' But she draws a blank. So the sweet young thing and her parents move hopefully down to the Commodore.

Here a small, darkish room is filled with young people: the bearded boys wearing polo-necked white shirts with their dinner jackets, the girls fragile in their extravagant hairpieces and thin evening pyjamas. The band plays novelty numbers. A jolly young man gets into difficulties with the Bossa Nova: 'Tell you what,' he says to the band, 'we'll start and you follow!' Some of the spectators wear Yacht Club gear. The sweet young thing dances rather reluctantly with her father and returns to her table, where her mother is discussing a mutual acquaintance with a female friend. 'No, Ann's girl never married. So pretty. But you know Ann – no young man was good enough for her daughter!' 'Mummy, take note!' says the sweet young thing self-consciously.

At midnight, the lights dim. Just outside a waiter lights twenty-one candles on a large cake with 'Happy Birthday Steve' traced on it with icing sugar. A musician, also called Steve, with a concertina strapped to his torso, has a quick glass of champagne: 'Where's the young man sitting?' he asks. The cake is wheeled in, followed by the musician playing 'Happy Birthday to You' and 'Twenty-one Today'. ('I've got the key of the door, Never been twenty-one before.') The birthday boy is fallen upon by his friends and tossed in the air twenty-one times. 'Hang on a sec – I think something went then!' A dishevelled figure, he is thrust on to the bandstand for a speech.

'I wanted my sister to be here to say what a fantastic bloke I am. But she couldn't get away. And I couldn't find anyone else to say I'm a fantastic bloke. So I'm a rotten bloke. But Ladies and Gentlemen, I want you to raise your glasses to my absent sister, who's my twin as a matter of fact, so it's her twenty-firster too . . . '

There is applause while the cake is cut and distributed. One of Steve's friends asks for 1000 pieces to be wrapped up and left with the hall porter on Sunday morning.

Upstairs, only Mrs Oakley-Ruck and Mrs Kramer are left in the ballroom: the orchestra has vanished. 'After midnight, it goes dead here,' says Mrs Oakley-Ruck. 'But on Sunday night they show a film. It was a perfectly putrid one last week, about the war. All dead bodies and blood . . . Oh, this hotel is easily the best in England. Of course, it's changed a lot since we've known it, much more modernised. But then hotels are changing everywhere. I shouldn't be surprised if Mr Clore owned them all now: he owns all the shops, doesn't he? But of course the Imperial's under *private* management.'

Mr Chapman, passing through the empty hall on his way to bed, has news of the burglary. 'The police think the man they want was seen on the six o'clock train back to Paddington. There are a lot of these specialised hotel thieves. This one lives in Spain, hops over here, visits hotels and takes the stuff back to Spain. Interpol know all about him. What they think he does is walk into the lounge at tea-time, listen as the guests give their room numbers to the waitress, then nip upstairs and rob the empty bedrooms. It's very easy to do – I've tried it myself in London hotels just to see. I mean, one can just walk upstairs and nobody knows one's not a guest.'

The couple with the young daughter come up from the night-club, leave orders with the night porter for early-morning tea and the Sunday papers, and disappear into the lift. The two ladies go on discussing hotels.

'They have very good food at the Branksome Tower in Bourne-mouth,' says Mrs Oakley-Ruck.

'It always seems rather sad to me,' says Mrs Kramer. '*Dated*, somehow. They have an old telephone booth there, and I can just imagine all the flappers ringing up for cocktails!'

'It may be patchy, but they've tried to modernise it.'

'Well, they've failed. I think it's dated.'

'So many hotels have gone downhill terribly, it's such a shame. They don't seem to bother somehow, it's odd. But the Palace at Babbacombe is nice – they've got a badminton court, oh, everything, but of course there's no sea view. And the Welcombe just outside Stratford used to be so pleasant, they took a *lot* of trouble. Lovely grounds – though I believe they're rather built over now. It's nice to see the old *Tatler* back again, isn't it?'

'I don't know, it seems to me rather dated. The *Illustrated London News* had an article about hotels – one in the Cotswolds, and the Westbury in Conduit Street.'

'I live near the Carlton Tower, but these American hotels in England aren't like the *real* American hotels. Not like the dear old Statler in Washington. Of course, my local's the Royal Court. I often go there, always have. You see, they *know* me there, which I always think makes all the difference, don't you?'

1968

189

HEATHCOTE WILLIAMS

I SOMETIMES ARGUE WITH MY FRIEND HEATHCOTE WILLIAMS about his use of pornography as a means of attacking his political enemies. It seems to me an irrelevant weapon in any context, and in the hands of a man with Heathcote's anarchistic, optimistic, nearly utopian convictions it becomes puzzlingly inconsistent. His polemical essays have been appearing, often unsigned, in the underground press over the past decade, and a selection, entitled *Severe Joy*, is listed for publication next year by John Calder. They abound in fantastic, and often very funny, descriptions of the people he disapproves of (such as Mrs Thatcher, Enoch Powell, Ian Paisley, the Royal Family and Jesus Christ) engaged in eccentric forms of sexual intercourse. One might almost assume from a few of these scatological diatribes that he thought there was something intrinsically disgusting and automatically degrading about physical love – and yet the opposite is the case. After all, he was a leading light at the Wet Dream Film Festival organised by *Suck* magazine in Amsterdam nine years ago, and I have heard him express the belief that human sperm contains psychedelic properties. To quote from the 278-year-old hero of his play *The Immortalist*: 'One of the purposes of love-making (not that you can make love – love *is*) is to achieve immortality . . . When it fails, you get conception.' This seems to imply, in its paradoxical fashion, that Heathcote sees the act of copulation as potentially mystical, perhaps even sacred. So why the emphasis on obscenity as a form of abuse? Isn't there some element of contradiction here? But my argument gets nowhere. Heathcote scowls prettily, tosses what can only be called his 'unruly curls', and accuses me of being an irredeemable media turd and a closet Monarchist.

The Immortalist is a wildly stimulating, mildly disturbing duologue in the form of a television interview with a man who refuses to die.

With the exception of myself and a few others of my ilk still circulating, every human being ever born on this planet has been murdered, consented to be murdered and spent their entire lives preparing for that pointless little spurt so beloved by footling existentialists. It's time for Life and Death to get divorced, maybug. What is more revolutionary than the conquest of death? Marxist-Leninist misery? Property is theft? I bet you two shillings to a toffee apple Proudhon couldn't nick a packet of spam out of Safeways.

I first read it two years ago, when Heathcote called round to see me with a typescript copy. On leaving my house, he was immediately arrested by two policewomen who (he claims) duffed him up and accused him of being drunk in charge of a bicycle. I found myself a key defence-witness at his trial, a long-drawn-out and solemn affair at the end of which he was acquitted. I first saw it acted a year later at the National Theatre of Frestonia – the name given to two streets in North Kensington which, threatened with demolition, had declared a sort of UDI in the manner of *Passport to Pimlico*. It has since been performed in various places, most recently at last month's Edinburgh Festival.

Visitors to the Festival also had the chance of seeing Heathcote play the part of Prospero in a film version of *The Tempest* directed by Derek Jarman. 'Isn't that bit about me breaking my staff and drowning my book supposed to be rather important?' he asked me. 'Well, Derek said he had trouble fitting it into his conception of the play and I think it's been cut.' Nonetheless, Heathcote's performance was praised in *The Listener* as 'melancholically smouldering' – and he might indeed be considered a kind of Prospero to the alternative society (although his personality contains a touch of Ariel's volatility, too, with possibly just a dash of Caliban's balefulness). Since his startling debut in 1964, when he was only twenty-three and his brilliant book *The Speakers* attracted the admiration of Harold Pinter, William Burroughs, Anthony Burgess, V. S. Pritchett and more, he has gradually achieved the status of super-wizard in a community of nomads, pilgrims and seekers after truth. For two years he successfully ran the Ruff, Tuff, Cream Puff Estate Agency (founded by Wat Tyler in 1381) which advised the homeless on suitable premises to squat. (I remember being taken aback, on receiving the agency's bulletin, to find my brother's house listed in it with the sinister comment: 'No apparent security between 11 and 12 p.m.') Soberly cycling round his domain on Notting Hill, surrounded by the peeling remnants of his own 'wall paintings' (graffiti which have long been accepted by local residents as permanent landmarks – 'Squat now while stocks last', 'A woman without a man is like a fish without a bicycle'), Heathcote seems to occupy the centre of a charmed circle.

His relationship to 'magic' is of two kinds. He is a skilled conjuror whose tricks have diverted many a geriatric ward (although an attempt to levitate his daughter China on the stage of the Lyttelton Theatre was less successful, and a defiant stab at fire-eating landed him with severe burns in a hospital bed beside a patient with gangrene of the testicles). But he is also receptive to magic in its more literal sense, apparently willing to believe in almost anything, from UFOs to the fairy photos that fooled Conan Doyle. With his Kirlian camera he has photo-graphed the aura of a 50p piece (Heathcote is no friend to metrication) and found that it resembles a congealed bat's fart. His restless intelligence makes him impatient with logic and he is drawn to overstatement by a genuine indignation mixed with a teasing sense of farce; he celebrates the irrational in a facetiously punning language with evangelical and apocalyptic overtones.

> Clean your spark-plugs, Nosferatu Nerdniks. Ye that are heavy-laden, rip off your clothes, rise up and bathe the world in light. The Recording Angel's got a polaroid. Where's the Kirlian clapper boy? Akashic flashers, unsheathe your auric fronds and let it all hang out so far you gotta pump air into it. Click. Click. Take *infinity*! . . . Crown King Thing. The aura bomb has been deton-ated. Our energy is continuous and immortal . . .

And so on – when he hits this vein, Heathcote can keep it up indefinitely. But in his best work – *The Speakers*, and four of his plays – the whimsical gift of the gab is disciplined by a basic sense of dramatic structure to produce an effect combining lethal accuracy of recorded speech with vertiginous imaginative flights. His study of the Hyde Park orators might have been taken as a masterly piece of reportage when it came out fifteen years ago; rereading it today, one can more easily recognise in it the germs of an exuberant creative gift. The critics who praised it so highly were far-seeing: it still has the staying power of a classic. (A dramatised version, staged in 1974, was worthy of the original.) Heathcote's first play, *The Local Stigmatic* (1965), is a short, chilling drama about two drop-outs obsessed to the point of unbalance by the media's fabrication of phoney celebrities; they recognise a minor actor in a pub, follow him out and savagely beat him up. This theme is elaborated in *AC/DC* (1970), a full-length play of dazzling invention and overwhelming power. Both works, considered obscure and unnecessarily violent by many people at the time, now seem to have been uncannily prophetic of the Manson murders. 'What were the Manson murders about?' said Heathcote in an interview.

> You could say they were about somebody trying to get his songs published: a grub under the blanket of the Great Society. The explanation is that there are two tribes: those who are under-nourished in terms of tribal approval, and those who are so overnourished that they become severely debilitated . . . The point is that Attention is a basic human need like food or sex. No child develops without it, and if you don't get it you wrinkle up. And as the media stand now .0001 per cent of the population is getting *crème brûlée* every day, and the rest are being ignored.

In *AC/DC* Heathcote furthered the investigation into the speech rhythms and thought patterns of schizophrenia which he had begun with the character of MacGuinness in *The Speakers*, unnervingly relating paranoid delusions of 'electronic control' to the actual developments in technological progress which underpin our lives. Ending with a trepanation scene performed onstage, it is a very frightening play, and perhaps it frightened Heathcote. Certainly *Hancock's Last Half Hour* (1977) – a witty, melancholy monologue leading up to the comedian's suicide in an Australian hotel room – reverts to a more humanist theatrical tradition; while *The Immortalist* recalls the dialectical device exploited by Diderot in *Le Neveu de Rameau*.

Since 1970, Heathcote's serious writing for the theatre has become marginally mellower in tone while his propaganda pieces grow more outrageously scabrous. At the time when he was inveighing against famous people as psychic capitalists getting their astral projection on the cheap, he fell in love with the most famous model in the world, Jean Shrimpton, and lived with her for several years. I assume that this item of personal history may be mentioned without impertinence, because Heathcote has published, next to a mutilated photograph of Jean, a virulent exercise in loathing called *Polythene Pam* which rivals Céline's lunatic ravings against the Jews in its intemperate nastiness. It is clear that what Heathcote hated was himself for ever having paused from hating what she represented.

So he is a creature of extremes. Of conventional upper-middle-class origin (educated at Eton; father a QC – 'just like Rumpole'; mother a clergyman's daughter), he excels at writing about alcoholics, schizophrenics, junkies, tramps. Accidentally contemporary with such movements as flower power and the drug culture, he became in a sense their Savonarola, embracing their cause with a passion, energy and rigour conspicuously lacking in their other devotees. Possessed of a remarkable intellect, he takes a perverse pleasure in giving credence to the most far-fetched rubbish he can find. Gentle and generous in life, he can be spiteful and violent in print. By the same token, endearingly muddled as a companion, he can rise in his plays to heights of piercing illumination that make one think of Rimbaud.

1979

THE KRAYS

PERHAPS MR PEARSON WILL FORGIVE ME IF I OPEN MY REVIEW of his book (*The Profession of Violence: The Rise and Fall of the Kray Twins* by John Pearson) on a personal note. Early in 1965, I was approached by the Kray twins, who invited me to write their biography: I believe that I was by no means the first journalist to whom this suggestion had been made. At that time, they were at the height of their apparent 'invincibility': they had just been acquitted after a widely publicised trial for demanding money with menaces; the *Daily Mirror* had been forced to print an apology to Ronnie Kray; they were beginning to be vaguely famous as 'gangsters'. Yet I understood their main motive for commissioning the book to be as an insurance against the inevitable day of their arrest, when it could be published and (as it was bound to be a bestseller) the proceeds would support their parents for the rest of their lives. They told me they wanted the book to be 'true – like Harold Robbins'. I had a series of interviews with them and with many of their friends. In the process I became fascinated by their personalities and the atmosphere that surrounded them in their East End kingdom, but found it almost impossible to establish coherent facts. Finally, I told them that I was incapable of producing a book that would simultaneously satisfy them, myself, the police and the reading public: but I remained in touch with them, and continued to visit them after they were arrested in 1968 and sentenced to life imprisonment the following year.

One night in 1967, I was woken by the telephone: a voice from a call-box told me that Ronnie wanted to see me urgently the next day. This, I thought with a sinking heart, is the crunch: friends had warned me that a time might come when the Krays would make a demand that I would dare neither obey nor refuse. The assignation was in the hall of the Regent Palace Hotel: a stranger approached me, led me to a car and, after a circuitous drive, into a basement flat. Ronnie was at this time going through a religious phase, combined with a craze for health food: there was only fruit juice to drink, while a record of the Lord's Prayer was playing on the gramophone. He told me that an American publisher was interested in the Kray biography, and had suggested a geezer called John Pearson as the writer. Was Pearson crooked or straight? 'Crooked' would have meant being an agent for the CID or FBI. Relieved, I was able to reassure him that Pearson was the distinguished author of two successful biographies, of Ian Fleming and Donald Campbell. The twins decided to trust Pearson. Later that year, they found him a flat near their family home in Bethnal Green, gave him extensive interviews and introduced him to those of their associates who were in favour and at large.

I think that, like me, Pearson was both fascinated by the atmosphere surrounding the twins and puzzled as to how to arrive at the truth behind it. After the arrests and long, expensive trials his task became easier – although difficulties must have remained to the end. The Krays could only be convicted on the evidence of people who were themselves (to put it mildly) not entirely reliable, and it is on such sources that he had to depend for much of the information in the book. While certain details in his narrative are open to question (I myself spotted a few minor inaccuracies, and people more closely involved have mentioned many more), there is no doubt that in all essentials his narrative outline is correct. His contract with the Krays (by which their mother shares in the book's profits) has enabled him to write openly about the twins, but a certain caution had to be preserved about other figures closely connected with their story. They thus emerge (possibly to their satisfaction) as superstars: isolated embodiments of murderous violence, somehow distinct from that criminal underworld which – in ambiguous relationship to society and the police – produced them, encouraged them to flourish and survives their downfall. My criticism of his book is that, by concentrating on the twins as outstanding personalities (however maleficent) independent of a sociological background, he creates a demand which he does not satisfy. The 'atmosphere' is missing – is this perhaps what they meant themselves when they invoked the name of Harold Robbins? John Pearson writes that they emerged from the trial as 'cardboard monsters' – and this is how they emerge from his book. Monsters they may be, but he must know they are far from cardboard.

This lack of vivid characterisation and psychological insight may not be Mr Pearson's fault. He told me, when we were both visiting the twins at Brixton, that he saw them as Dostoevskian figures: and his first version of the book had the suggestive title of *The Brothers Kray*. This version, however, was rejected by Jonathan Cape as being insufficiently dramatic: and it is a second version which eventually found another publisher. I suspect that the first may have been the better. However, I do not agree with him about Dostoevsky: in my view, the only writer who could have done them neither less nor more than justice is Dickens. He would have responded to, and conveyed, the unnerving mixture of terror, sentimentality and humour that characterised their careers. Mr Pearson refers to Reggie's 'charm', but fails to illustrate it, and Ronnie's bouts of madness are described in conventional terms of compassionate horror which fail to evoke its essence. Dickens would have disapproved of the Krays so profoundly that one can imagine him insisting on the restoration of the death penalty on their behalf, but he would have understood the bewildering contradictions in their natures: their rigid conformity coupled with an inability to see the world except in criminal terms, their cosy gift of friendship overshadowed by their terrifying suspiciousness, their shallow emotionalism punctuated by sudden, illogical outbursts of destruction and despair. And such an understanding might have led to a glimpse of the mystery of criminal violence – which must presumably be the main aim of writing about the Krays.

Mr Pearson is no Dickens, and neither am I, so my suggestions may strike him as impertinent. I wish, however, that he had devoted more space to Violet Kray, the twins' mother, whom he correctly, but inadequately, describes as 'strong-willed, romantic and possessive'. The gangster's mother is a cliché figure, usually presented in the movies as a white-haired crone dressed in black and invoking the Holy Virgin in a Sicilian accent. Mrs Kray has a potent domestic charm: both 'down-to-earth' and dignified, she is the most indulgent person I have ever met, turning even so harrowing an occasion as visiting her sons in the top-security wing at Parkhurst into a privileged adventure, punctuated by a series of little treats in the form of a cup of tea, a bag of chips, a rye-bread sandwich.

There is something indefinably 'special' about her. She told me once that, as a young woman, she had longed to travel but had assumed she would never be able to afford it. Since then, she has enjoyed several holidays in Majorca – 'and I owe that,' she added proudly,'to Reg and Ron.' The key to the Krays is in their view of themselves, and this must be a legacy, distorted to hideous proportions, from her. They always felt 'special': they still do. Reg once said to me: 'Psychiatrists and that are always arguing about the criminal mentality. There's no mystery. If you haven't got an education, and if you want to make something of yourself, what else can you do? There's only boxing other than crime, and you can't do that for long.' John Pearson's book shows how, to 'make something of themselves' in crime, they had to invoke fear. (Their term for it was 'respect' – not wholly inaccurate in the context.) When the opportunity came to graduate to the higher, more truly respectable (because exclusively financial) echelons of crime, they failed to make the transition, clinging to the primitive concept of 'respect' which they reinforced by brutal and almost motiveless murders. This book will not alter their view of themselves: it may even strengthen it. They are now in the ironic position of disliking the book itself, but hoping that it will be widely read. Their objections to it are revealing of their widely different characters – for in spite of being identical twins, they are in many respects opposites. Reg is distressed at the implication that he was resonsible for the suicide of his wife, whom he still adores. Ron took umbrage at a remark that his murder of George Cornell was 'the worst-kept secret in the East End': 'I didn't mean it to be a secret. If I'd wanted nobody to know about it, I'd have done it clever-like, wouldn't I?'

In dramatising their story, John Pearson has inevitably had to simplify it. He presents Ronnie as a homosexual psychopath, sustained by lunatic fantasies of power which he eventually turns into dangerous reality, dragging along with him a reluctant Reggie, who if left to himself might have been a brilliant businessman but who is destroyed by the fatal state of twinship. Certainly, Ronnie's character contains features which might be considered eccentric even within the context of the criminal underworld, while Reggie's is comparatively rational. But to me they are mainly interesting because the motive power behind their rise always contained the seeds of their even more spectacular fall. They wanted to be famous, at the centre of a myth, like Al Capone, like Jesse James. In this they were amateurish: the professional criminal does not draw attention to his activities. They lived in a world of nightmare, one aspect of which was that the fame they sought inevitably caused their ruin and disgrace. This book, which they themselves inspired but over which they lost control, at the same time deepens their disgrace and perpetuates their fame.

1972

EATING ALONE

SOMETIMES, WHEN I AM ALONE IN THE EVENINGS AND FEEL like giving myself a treat, I go to a little restaurant round the corner called the Star of Bombay. An old newspaper cutting is displayed in its window containing a guarded recommendation by Fay Maschler, but in spite of this the place is nearly always empty. Occasionally a transient figure may appear, swiftly and rather furtively, to carry off a take-away ordered earlier by telephone. Two young Indian waiters in dinner jackets hover apprehensively at the back of the room, while behind and above them, seated on a raised platform, a somewhat older Indian lady regally presides. To an impressionable customer, she can suggest both the motherly authority of Indira Gandhi and the unbridled licence of erotic Hindu art.

The walls are lined by banquettes to accommodate ten tables for four; one further table, seating only two, has been placed near the centre. Its exposed situation gives it a rickety appearance, and when I am invariably and firmly escorted to it by a waiter I often mutinously wonder why I cannot sit, in solitary splendour, at one of the vacant larger tables – but the feeling of awe inspired in me by the lady has hitherto prevented me from voicing the request. I order Vegetable Biryani and a salted Lassi; two Papadams are provided whether I ask for them or not. This meal costs exactly four pounds, to which a service supplement of forty pence is added on the bill.

Once I made the mistake of bringing a book with me, to help pass the time between the ordering of the food and its arrival, which can be as long as twenty minutes. It was Anita Brookner's novel *Look At Me*. The sight of a man sitting on his own and reading a book must have struck the lady as in some way peculiar and worthy of investigation, for she descended from her dais and gracefully approached the little table. 'I see you are very, very deep in that book,' she said, giggling gently. 'I expect it must be a very nice book. I am very interested in books myself, you see. Let me see what is it is called!' She took it from my grasp and inspected it closely. *'Look At Me*! I think that is a very funny title. I expect it is a very funny book. And I expect you are very fond of reading.' She returned it to me and, chuckling to herself, went back to her seat.

For some time after this, as soon as I entered the Star of Bombay, the lady would come down from her vantage-point into the well of the room to greet me. 'Ah, here is the nice man who is so fond of reading! How are you getting on with *Look At Me*? Have you finished it yet? Does it have a happy ending? Why did you not bring a book with you tonight?' I had almost decided to try and find an alternative restaurant (though I knew there could not be another so near and so good and so cheap) when she at last lost interest in my reading habits and left me alone. I too must have forgotten the incident, for one night, obeying an impulse to dine at the Star of Bombay, I thoughtlessly snatched up a paperback before setting out. As I neared the dimly-lit façade, with the inviting credit-card symbols surrounding the ragged and by now illegible newspaper cutting in the window, I suddenly remembered that my book was a novel by Anne Tyler called *Dinner at the Homesick Restaurant*.

The lady must never see this. I managed to conceal it under my coat until, while settling myself at the table, I slipped it onto the chair and sat down on top of it. An uneasy sense of subterfuge must have made me more than normally clumsy, for as I executed this manoeuvre I also knocked over the slender glass vase which stood beside an ashtray on the paper tablecloth. It rolled to the edge, spilling a little water as it did so, then fell to the floor, decapitating the single tulip that it had nurtured but suffering no injury itself. This minor accident might have passed unnoticed in a busy restaurant; at the Star of Bombay, it caused a commotion. The waiters fussed about my table, solemn and solicitous; the lady paid me a brief visit, to convey a message of concern, amusement and forgiveness. I squirmed in my seat, inadvertently ruffling the pages of the clandestine paperback beneath me.

Having given my regular order, I prepared to sit out the waiting period in an enjoyable reverie. But the street door opened, and two men made a noisy and dramatic entrance. The elder was over sixty, unusually large, with thick white hair and a round, clean-shaven face. His companion was about ten years younger and almost as powerfully built, with a bald head and a dark beard. Their massive physiques were augmented by their bulky clothing: I had a confused impression of woollen shirts, knitted ties, tweed jackets, flannel and corduroy trousers, cardigans, pullovers, sweaters, parkas, anoraks, mufflers and capacious fur-trimmed overcoats.

The elder man stood for a while by the door surveying the room and raising his hands in a kind of blessing. 'Perfect. Lovely. Yes. Exactly right. Brilliant idea.' One of the waiters gingerly approached him. 'A very good evening to you, sir,' said the white-haired man. 'Could you possibly oblige us with a table for two? You can? Oh, how lovely. Most courteous of you. My friend and I are exceedingly beholden to you. This evening, you see, is in the nature of a special occasion . . . Most kind. No, if it's all the same to you, sir, I think we might find ourselves more comfortable at this one.' To my horror, he had picked the table nearest to mine.

The process of partially undressing and then deliberately installing themselves at this table took a very long time; while it was going on, the younger man repeated my own mishap, and upset the vase and the tulip at his elbow. 'I hate people who never knock things over,' boomed his companion. 'Can't abide 'em. They're so *boring*. I can't stand boredom, never could. Life's too short.' The waiter retrieved the vase from the floor and replaced it, with its battered flower, on the table. 'Oh, I say, sir, that's uncommonly civil of you. Now, sir, if you'd be so good as to give us a little time to ponder the bill of fare, we'll be ready to place our orders in a minute or two. But hold hard – *drink*. Manfred, what say you?'

'Oh, lager's favourite with me when I'm eating Indian,' said his friend.

'Then lager it shall be. Two lagers, please, my dear fellow.'

'Two pints of lager,' confirmed the waiter.

'No, no . . . half-pints, half-pints. There's something rather crude about a pint glass, don't you find?' He looked vaguely round the room, as if expecting applause, and then his gaze confronted mine. 'Pray tell me, sir, will you be requiring your ashtray? No? Sensible man – wish I had your strength of mind. That's really very handsome of you,' he went on, accepting it from my hands, 'very handsome of you indeed.'

The white-haired man ceremoniously positioned the ashtray beside him and then leant across and gave Manfred an affection-ate pinch on his bearded cheek. 'I say, my dear fellow, this *is* a lovely reunion. Queer, isn't it, the way a bundle of banknotes can make all the difference to an occasion?'

'You're looking much fitter than last time,' said Manfred. 'I scarcely knew you. Lost a lot of weight.'

'I don't eat, you see. That's the secret of losing weight. Well, I *eat* – but not like I used to do once upon a time.'

'I really mean it. You look years younger.'

The waiter brought their drinks, and they turned to study the menu. The older man now assumed a joke Indian accent, of the kind popularised by Peter Sellers in the early 1960s. 'Well I never, they have Bangladeshi Fruit Salad, that is very nice indeed.' In his normal voice, he continued: 'Right – well, we will most certainly sample your King Prawn Curry, for a start.'

'As a starter, sir?'

'No, no, not as a starter – for a *start*.'

'How many, sir?'

'Two. And I seem to remember finding the Rogan Josh rather tasty, so bring us two of that as well, if you would. Now, Manfred, dear fellow, what's the word on Meat Dopiaza?'

'Or perhaps Meat Korma Shah,' mused Manfred.

'I'm with you. We'll have two Dopiazas and two Korma Shahs. Oh, and we'll be wanting some Nan and Chapatis . . . '

'How many, sir?'

'Let's say, four Nan and six Chapatis. Then we needn't bother you again by asking for more. And that runny stuff – Raita – two go's of that, if you please. And what would an Indian meal be without my old friend Bhindi Bhaji?'

'Any rice, sir?'

'By all means. Two lots of Pilau Rice. Don't go away just yet, my dear fellow . . . I also want you to bring us some Sag Bhaji. Got that? Two Bhindi Bhajis and two Sag Bhajis. Plus a double portion of Vegetable Biryani – must have a vegetable dish or we might get scurvy! And now, would you say that that was enough for us? Remember, this is a celebration.'

I expected the waiter to tell him that they had ordered much too much, but he kept silent. In a low voice, Manfred said: 'Tikka.'

'Chicken? My dear fellow, of *course*.'

'Chicken Tikka,' said the waiter. 'How many?'

'Two. Two. Beautiful. I'm mightily in your debt, sir. My compliments to the chef, and tell him that's all we need – short of a phone call from your wife, eh, Manfred?' The white-haired man let out a roar of laughter.

It was impossible for me not to hear his monologue after this, but I did my best, by an effort of concentration, to avoid understanding its import. Nonetheless, a few phrases penetrated every defence and lodged in my consciousness. 'And the next thing I knew, there were torches shining in my eyes – nasty sensation, torchlight in your eyes. I don't recommend it – hadn't the foggiest notion where I was – middle of the night, but I didn't seem to be at home in bed – there were three of them – policemen, you see, that's what they were – are you squatting here or what, one of them wanted to know – I said, my good sir, you'll kindly watch your language when you're addressing me – didn't seem to mind – oh, they were all very good to me – I think what they thought was, we're all in the same boat really, it's just that he's gone one way and we've gone another – yes, I think that's what they must have felt.'

At about this point, one of the waiters brought my Vegetable Biryani and salted Lassi while the other produced two enormous helpings of Chicken Tikka for my neighbours.

'How good of you, sir. Most kind. Oh, this looks lovely. I must say, I haven't the foggiest recollection of ordering it, but no matter.'

Manfred muttered something.

'Of course – it was your bright idea. Brilliant. I say, this *is* a lovely reunion.'

'I didn't realise it was going to be such a lot,' said Manfred.

The lady herself now came to their table, bearing two outsize dishes piled high with some steaming substance which I could not identify. The talkative man fell silent at the sight of them;

he began to look a little worried. I knew that I would never be able to bear the embarrassment of witnessing *his* embarrassment when the rest of their gargantuan dinner arrived. I asked for my bill, and gobbled as much of my food as I could swallow until it came. I did not have the exact sum so I placed a five-pound note on the saucer (leaving a princely gratuity of sixty pence) and made my escape – just in time, for as I reached the exit I was aware of a procession of curries approaching the table of Manfred and his friend.

Hurrying home, I was almost at the corner of the street where I lived when I felt a tap on my shoulder. I turned, to find one of the waiters from the Star of Bombay behind me. 'Excuse me, sir, but I think you forgot something,' he said, handing me *Dinner at the Homesick Restaurant*.

1984

ACKNOWLEDGMENTS

'The Theatre of Embarrassment', 'P. J. Proby', 'The Embarrassment of Being Eamonn', 'The Sub-Cinema', 'Hylda at Home', 'Love Duet', 'The Discreet Charm of Stéphane Audran', 'Gloria Grahame', 'Brando', 'The Pearly King', 'Mother and Son', 'Camera Club' and 'The Imperial Hotel, Torquay' were first published in *The Sunday Times Magazine* and are reprinted by kind permission. Of the remaining pieces, all but two first appeared in the following publications: *The New Statesman*, *The Listener*, *The London Review of Books*, *Encounter*, *The Times Literary Supplement*, *The London Magazine* and *The Spectator*.